Learning to Think

Jan Black, Author

Steve Hunt and Dave Adamson, Design and Illustration

We, the people who made this book, like to help kids learn to think.

And the One who helped all of us was God, Who wants even more than we do to help you learn to think.

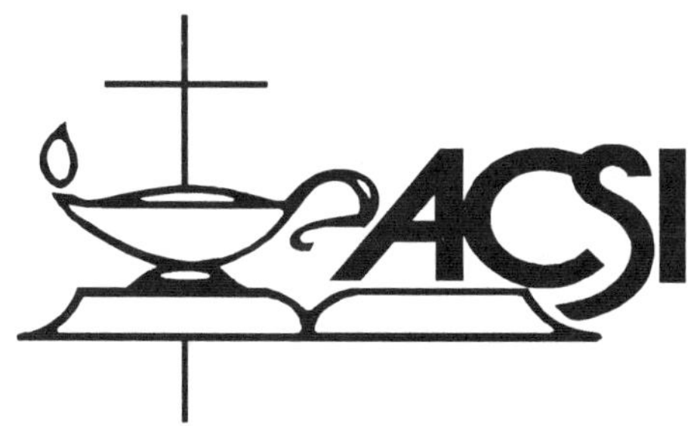

A Publication of

ASSOCIATION OF CHRISTIAN SCHOOLS INTERNATIONAL

P.O. Box 35097 Colorado Springs, Colorado 80935-3509

NOTE: In order to make all references to God clear to students, we have chosen to capitalize pronouns referring to deity rather than follow the uncapitalized form of the NIV.

Table of Contents

BERTA RIBBLE
DONALD WHEELER
T.J. FLANDERS
MARTA RIBBLE
JEANNE CARLIN
Sunnyview Christian School
MARTIN MAGEE
MRS. NELL SHIPPS
MISS NORA KIRK
MR. LEO QUINN
2nd Graders are GREAT!
TAMBI McNUTT
MR. EDMUND BELLO

You are on the BRINK of learning to THINK!

Are you a thinker? Then this book is for you . This book will help you train your mind to think right about life.

Thinking right about life is one of the smartest things you can learn to do. Thinking right about life is what God wants for you. God is on your side and wants you to live a life that makes you glad to be you.

Shopping For Thoughts

Lists are handy. Some moms take lists to the store to help them choose what to buy. God put this handy list in the Bible to help us choose what thoughts to think. He said that it is best for us to think about things that are:

1. True
2. Noble
3. Right
4. Pure
5. Lovely
6. Admirable
7. Excellent
8. Praiseworthy

Some of these words are big. Their meaning is big, too.
We will talk more about them later.

What Do You Think?

Out of all the things that we can do, what two count the most to God?

1. ______________________________

2. ______________________________

Some people asked Jesus to tell them what things God most wants us to do. This was His answer:

1 Thing to Do: ______________________________.

2 Thing to Do: ______________________________, including ______________________________

It is good for your mind to know this. It is kind of God to tell us what He wants us to do.

How? How? How?

Let your mind think of a way to show you love God the most.

Let your mind think of a way to show you love people.

Let your mind think of a way to show you love yourself.

Is your mind tired?
Good! That means it is working!

Wisdom means
Thinking God's Way
instead of thinking like a fool.

God says, "She (Wisdom) is more precious than rubies, and nothing you desire can compare with her."
Proverbs 3:15

Precious = very special.

If I think God's way about Wisdom, I will work at getting

____

(things or wisdom?)

more than

____

(things or wisdom?)

Precious Wisdom

Rubies are red;
Sapphires are blue.
Wisdom's worth more
Than either of you.

Color one jewel red and the other one blue. Then color the rest of the space the color you think of when you think of wisdom.

This man wants to be rich more than anything.

This man wants to be wise more than anything.

Draw a line from here ☐ to the man with the most wisdom.

What Do You Think?

Can a wise man be rich? Yes No
Can a poor man be foolish? Yes No
Can a foolish man be wise? Yes No

THINKING TOGETHER

Parents:
In class we are busy looking at wisdom. We have learned that 1) she is precious, 2) she is from God, 3) she will help us think right about life, and 4) she will love us if we love her. For the child who learns to exercise wisdom, the potential for success in the matters of life is dramatic. We hope you enjoy thinking together about wisdom and that you will be strengthened in your belief of her beauty and practicality.

We all need wisdom. Parenting is tough. So is teaching. And being a child has its rough spots, too. Wisdom is available to us, so let's ask for her help – for ourselves and for one another.

The Baby's Wise Family

When I think wisely, it shows in what I do.
I can learn to see wisdom in other people.
The mother of Moses had wisdom. So did his big sister.

1. Moses was born to Father ____________ Mother ____________, Sister ____________ and Brother ____________,

2. It was a scary time to be born because the King wanted all of the boy babies killed.
   What kind of baby do you think mothers and fathers were hoping to have?
   Girls ☐ Boys ☐

3. Mother did not want her baby boy to die. She hid him until he was too big and loud to be hidden. She made a basket that would float.
   Think about how hard it would be to make a basket like that.
   ____
   How long do you think it would take? ____________

4. She sent the basket with sister ____________ to the river.
   Do you think it looked like she was going to the river for a picnic? Yes ☐ No ☐

5. Miriam put the basket into the river at just the right time. The king's daughter was taking a bath in the river. She saw the basket and asked her fancy helpers to get it for her.
   Do you think the mother and sister of Moses were hoping this would happen?
   Yes ☐ No ☐

6. The princess looked inside the basket. Moses cried. Her heart felt bad for the little Hebrew baby.

WHAT HAPPENED NEXT?

Think about God watching Moses and his family.
Mother waiting at home.
Miriam's heart racing as she ran home.
The wisdom of Moses' family.

They Chose Wisdom

Thinking back

- Mr. McShane was fixing the slide / swing / teeter totter
- Who found his wallet? Tambi / Patsy / Berta / Marta
- How hard was it to give back the wallet?

Find the first letter of the name of each girl who found the wallet. Put the first letter of each of the names on this line where you think it belongs.

______________	______________	______________
Very easy to give it back	Sort of easy to give it back	Very hard to give it back

How hard would it be for you to give back a wallet full of money? Put the first letter of your name where it fits on the line.

The girls let wisdom help them choose right. Choosing wisdom is not always easy, but it is always right.

What if?

What if the girls had been foolish?

They would have
- kept some of the money.
- never given the wallet back.
- kept all of the money and left the wallet there.

Someday I will find something that I want that belongs to someone else. Here is what I will do:

Here is what I will do

____

____

Thinking True

What is true?

True is something that really, really, really is.
True is something you can believe.

What is true of you?

I have ______________ hair and ______________ eyes.

My arms are ______________ inches long. My neck is ______________ around.

My favorite animal is ______________________________.

One other true thing about me is ______________________________
____.

What is true of God?

He owns the world. He cannot do wrong.
His word, the Bible, is true.
He wants you to be His friend.

One other true thing about God is ______________________________
____.

Thinking true is wise and smart.

A Smiling Thought

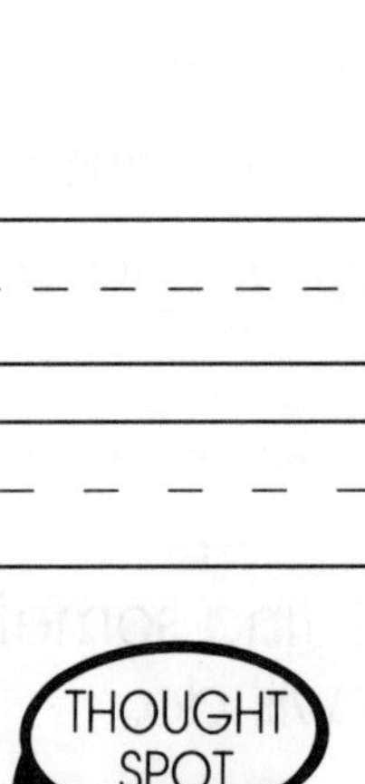

1. Think of God smiling at you.
2. Think of wisdom smiling at you, too.
3. Think of you holding hands with God and wisdom on a walk.
4. This is not a pretend thought. God says that He and wisdom will go with you and help you to choose right if you ask them.

Obedience means doing what I am told instead of not doing what I am told.

God says, "The wise in heart accepts commands, but a chattering fool comes to ruin."
Proverbs 10:8

Chattering = fast and foolish talking
Ruin = destroyed

If I think God's way about **obedience**, I will just do what I am told without making excuses or begging to get out of it.

There Were Three

Miss Kirk said, "I need to leave the room for a minute. I will hurry back. Please work quietly."

What happened?

T.J. Nikolas Donald Jeanne Martin Suzanne Julia Mae	sat at teacher's desk. shot a spitwad. threw an eraser. threw it back. guarded the door. did their work.

How would you have changed this story?
How do teachers know when these things happen?

What if?

What if Miss Kirk had come back 22 seconds before she did?
What if the whole class had thought right about obeying?
What if no one gives you a reward for doing right?

Here is what I will do

The next time my teacher leaves the room I will ______________________

____.

THINKING TOGETHER.

Parents:
You have just read the remains of a Sunnyview story. It is one way we are learning to think about obedience. Perhaps your child will fill you in on the details of the story. You may also want to ask to hear a poem about 4 billion people and 92.

Learning to obey is a lifetime project. As we work together on Phase One with your child, let's instruct with patience, understanding, and a good memory!

The Plan

1. Moses was a shepherd for his wife's dad. He was spending his time with sheep and rocks and trees. Sheep, rocks and trees do not talk, so Moses had lots of time to think.

   When is your best thinking time?

or

---

2. One day Moses and the sheep were near a mountain. God was there. God made himself into a burning bush and called to Moses. How could He do that? I think He could do that because

Would you go near a talking, burning bush?
Yes ☐ **No** ☐

---

3. God told Moses His plan to rescue the Hebrews in Egypt. God said He wanted Moses to go back to the king and tell him to let the Hebrews go.

   Pretend you are Moses. Let your mind take you to the mountain.

Is the [fire] crackling? Yes☐ No☐
Are the [sheep] baaa-ing or still?

Is the sky [sun] or [clouds] ?

Are you afraid? Yes ☐ No ☐

4. God told Moses the words to say to the King and to the Hebrews. Moses obeyed even though the plan made him nervous.

I think

I think it is sometimes hard to obey. Yes ☐ No ☐

A simple thing to obey would be .

A hard thing to obey would be .

I think God wants me to obey every person who tells me what to do. Yes☐ No☐

I think I would have liked to have been on the mountain with God and Moses. Yes☐ No☐

It All Adds Up

"The wise in heart accepts commands, but a chattering fool comes to ruin." Proverbs 10:8

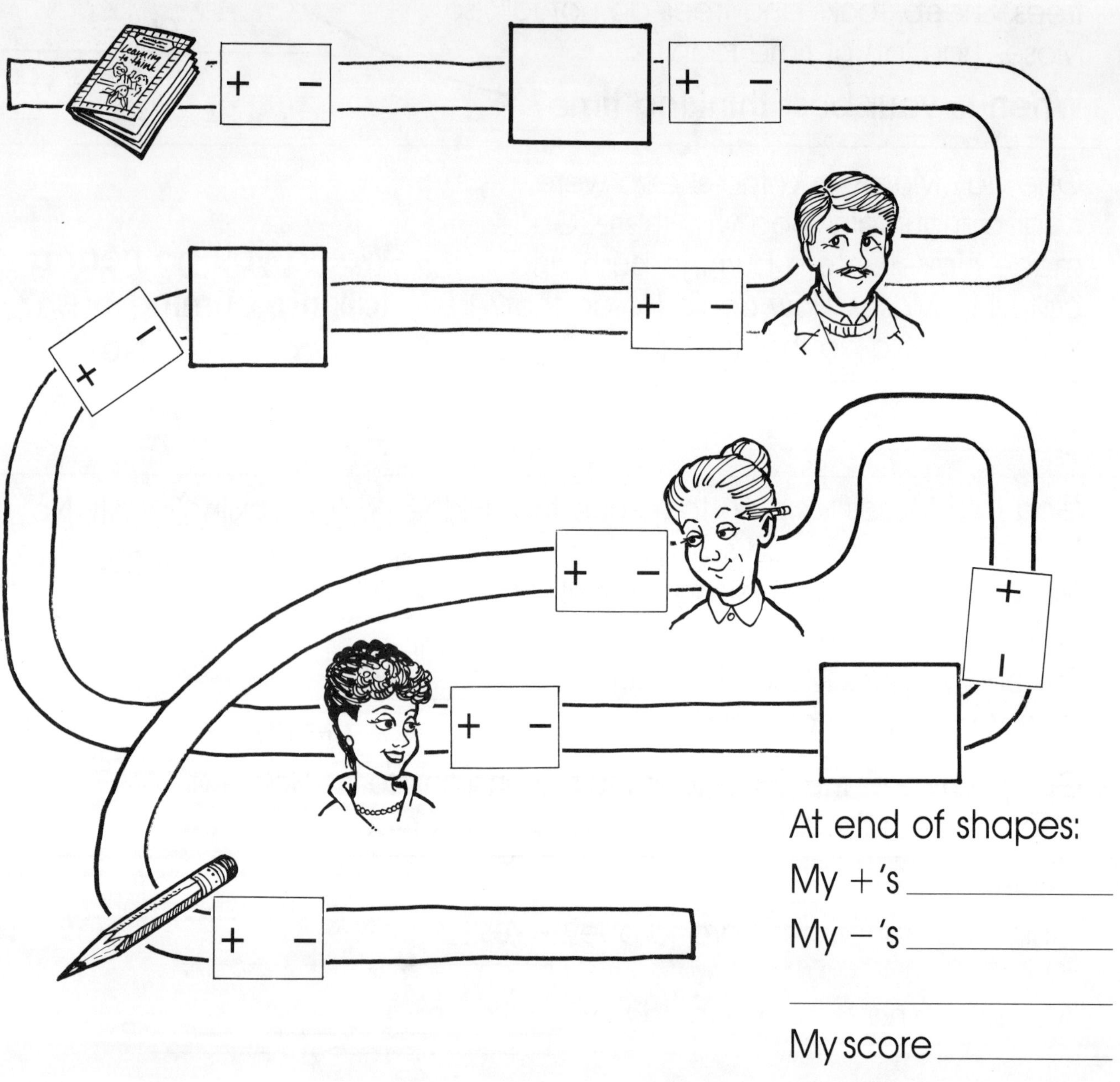

At end of shapes:

My +'s ____________

My –'s ____________

____

My score ____________

Just think, God is adding up all the times you obey. When you get to heaven, you will get to see your score! What do you think your score will be?

____

If

If 4 billion people and 92
Did what they were supposed to do,
The earth would surely get a reward
For showing such love to our
wonderful Lord.

If you and I, and just we two,
Did what we were supposed to do,
Then we would surely get a reward
For showing such love to our
wonderful Lord.

If I, just I, and not even two
Did what I was supposed to do,
Then I would surely get a reward
For showing such love to my
wonderful Lord!

A True Thought

In your mind, think of God smiling and handing you a reward for doing what you were told to do.

Now think of you giving your reward as a thank you gift to Jesus.

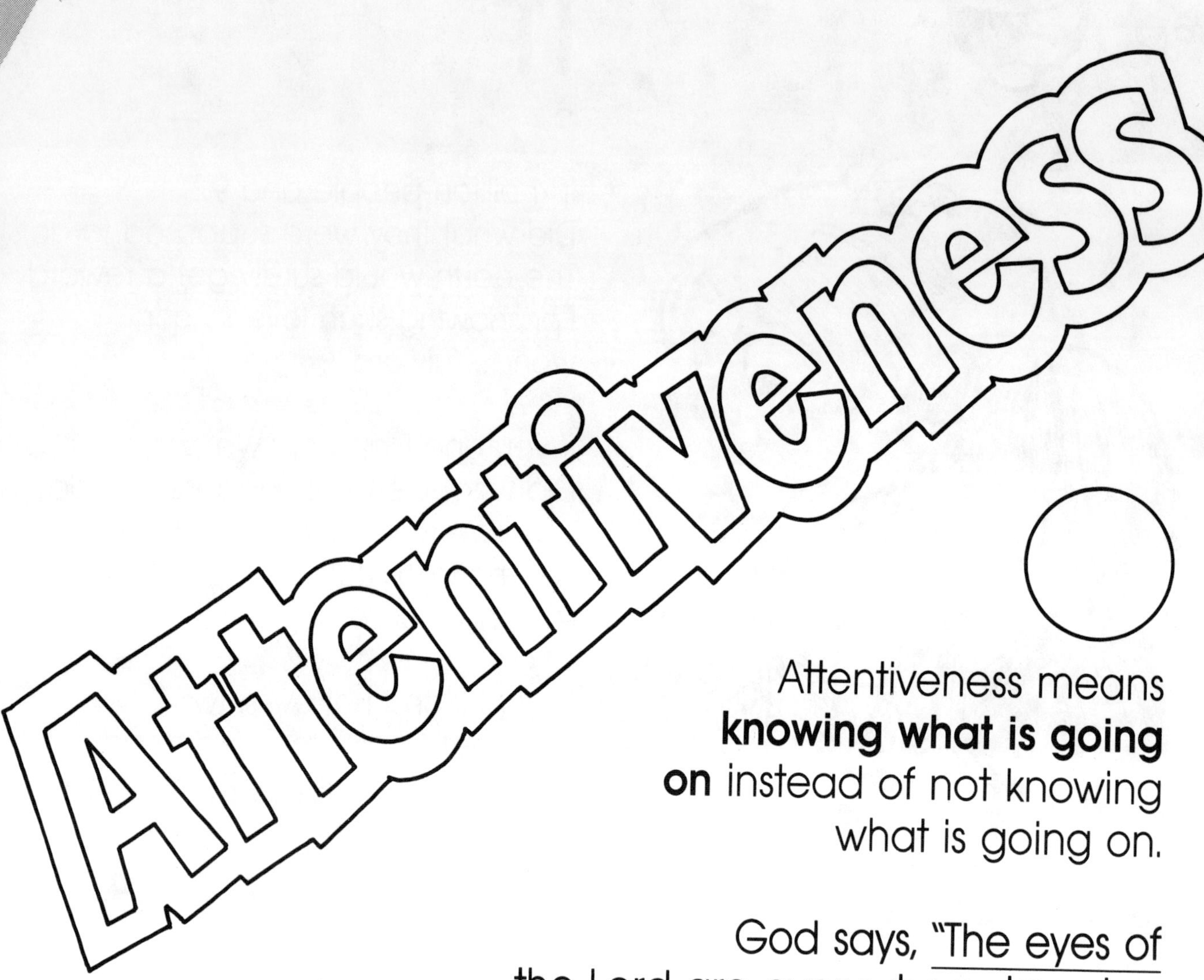

Attentiveness means **knowing what is going on** instead of not knowing what is going on.

God says, "The eyes of the Lord are everywhere, keeping watch on the wicked and the good." Proverbs 15:3

Wicked = Very, very bad

If I think God's way about **attentiveness**, I will remember God is paying attention to me,and I will pay attention to what is going on.

Who is Paying Attention to What?

1. Pay attention to this picture.
2. Now pay attention to the words.
3. Draw a line from the word box to the matching picture.

Who is paying attention:

- ☐ to the bird?
- ☐ to Miss Kirk?
- ☐ to the girls?
- ☐ to the skinned knee?
- ☐ to the swinger?
- ☐ to his thoughts?

THINKING TOGETHER.

Parents: For the next two weeks our class will be learning to pay attention, to notice what is going on. This is a critical skill for feeling good about ourselves and our environment. We also feel more secure when we are aware of what is happening.

So, as we join together to show your child the benefits of paying attention, let's not forget the power of a good example.

He Remembered It All!

A True Story BIBLE PAGE

1. Moses listened to every word God spoke.
   Which voice do you think God used?
   His thunder voice ________ His whisper voice ________
   His talking voice ________ His silent voice ________

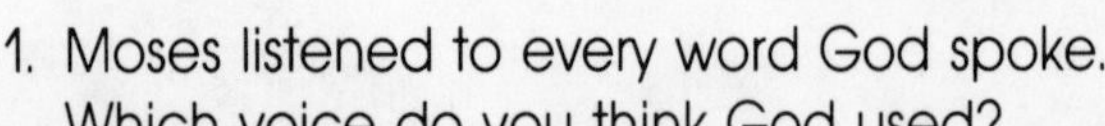

2. Moses asked God questions to be sure he knew what God meant. It is wise and smart to ask questions.
   What question will you ask God?
   ____

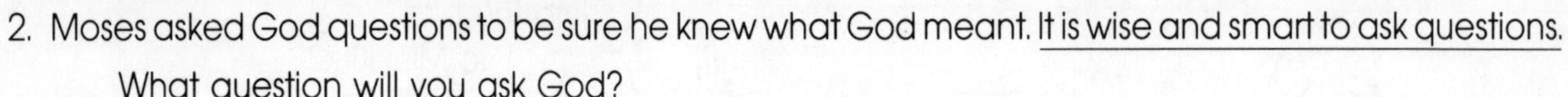

3. God told Moses what to do and say back home in Egypt. Some things were to be said to the Hebrews. Some things were to be said to the King. Moses paid attention. How many of them can you remember?

______ ______ ______ ______ ______ ______ ______ ______ ______ ______ ______ ______

IT TOOK TIME FOR THE KING TO LET THE HEBREWS GO

a. Pretend the plagues are on a clock.
b. Look at the picture of each plague.
c. Pay attention to the thoughts the plague puts into your mind.
   How does it feel?
   How does it sound?
   What do you see?
d. After you have done this, draw a line from the plague to the center of the clock.

"The eyes of the LORD are everywhere, keeping watch on the wicked and the good."
Proverbs 15:3

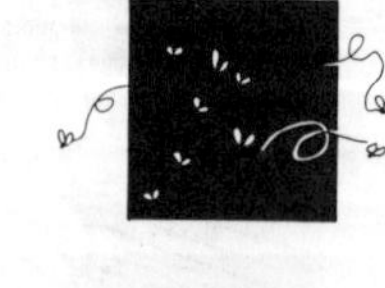

Feel it.
Hear it.
See it.

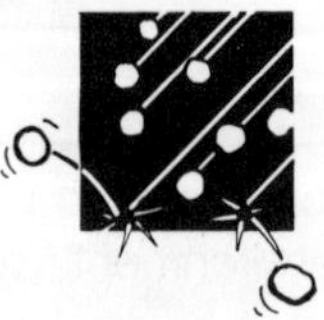

The Missed Hands

Thinking back

Mr. Quinn told the classes how to play the game. Here is what he said:

"First, put the nerf ball between your ______________.
knees, teeth

"Next, hop down to your ______________.
friend, teacher

"Tap your teacher's ______________.
hand, elbow

"Then run back to your team and give the ball to the next ______________."
person who calls you, person in line.

HERE'S WHAT HAPPENED

With your pencil or as many crayons as you think you need, draw what happened at recess. Show the hops and runs of each class. Remember how many missed the hand in Mr. Quinn's class.

Each class had 18 players.

MISS KIRK'S CLASS

The line

MR. QUINN'S CLASS

The line

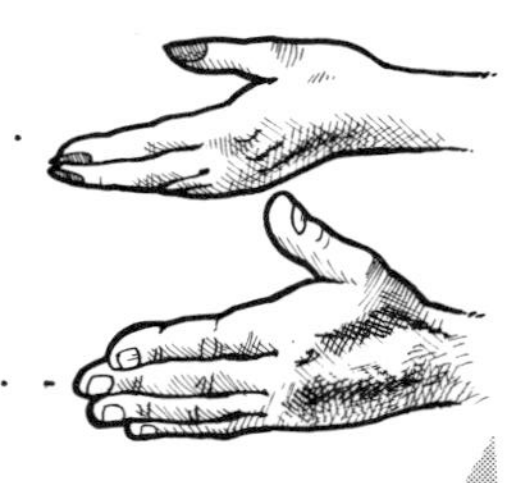

What if?

What if Mr. Quinn had not noticed that five hands didn't touch him?

What if he had not told Miss Kirk?

Here is what I will do

When someone notices something my team did not do the right way, I will: ______________

What Am I Missing?

What am I missin'
When I don't pay attention?
Maybe some news
That is too new to mention.
Maybe an answer that is said only once.
Maybe a question like, "Will you share my lunch?"
Maybe the scoop on the latest invention.

"Shhhhhhh… please be quiet.
I'm paying attention!"

- What news have you heard today?
- What answer was given only once?
- What question did someone ask you?
- What invention have you used today?

Have you ever asked someone to be quiet so you could pay attention? Yes No

Is it all right to ask someone to be quiet so you can pay attention? Yes No

Thinking Noble

Noble thoughts are special thoughts. Here is one:

"I think I will let Nikolas use my bat while I am at the dentist."

Here is another one:

"I've noticed that Mrs. Mason works hard, but she still smiles at us. I think I'll bring her a flower for her desk."

Here is a very, very noble thought:

"God is watching me. I will do right so He will be glad to be watching me."

FAITH
means
BELIEVING GOD
instead of Doubting God.

God says, "Believe in the Lord Jesus, and you will be saved." Acts 16:31

If I think God's way about FAITH,
I will trust Jesus to make a home for me in heaven.

Frog

Thinking back

Where do you think Frog went after the jar tipped over?

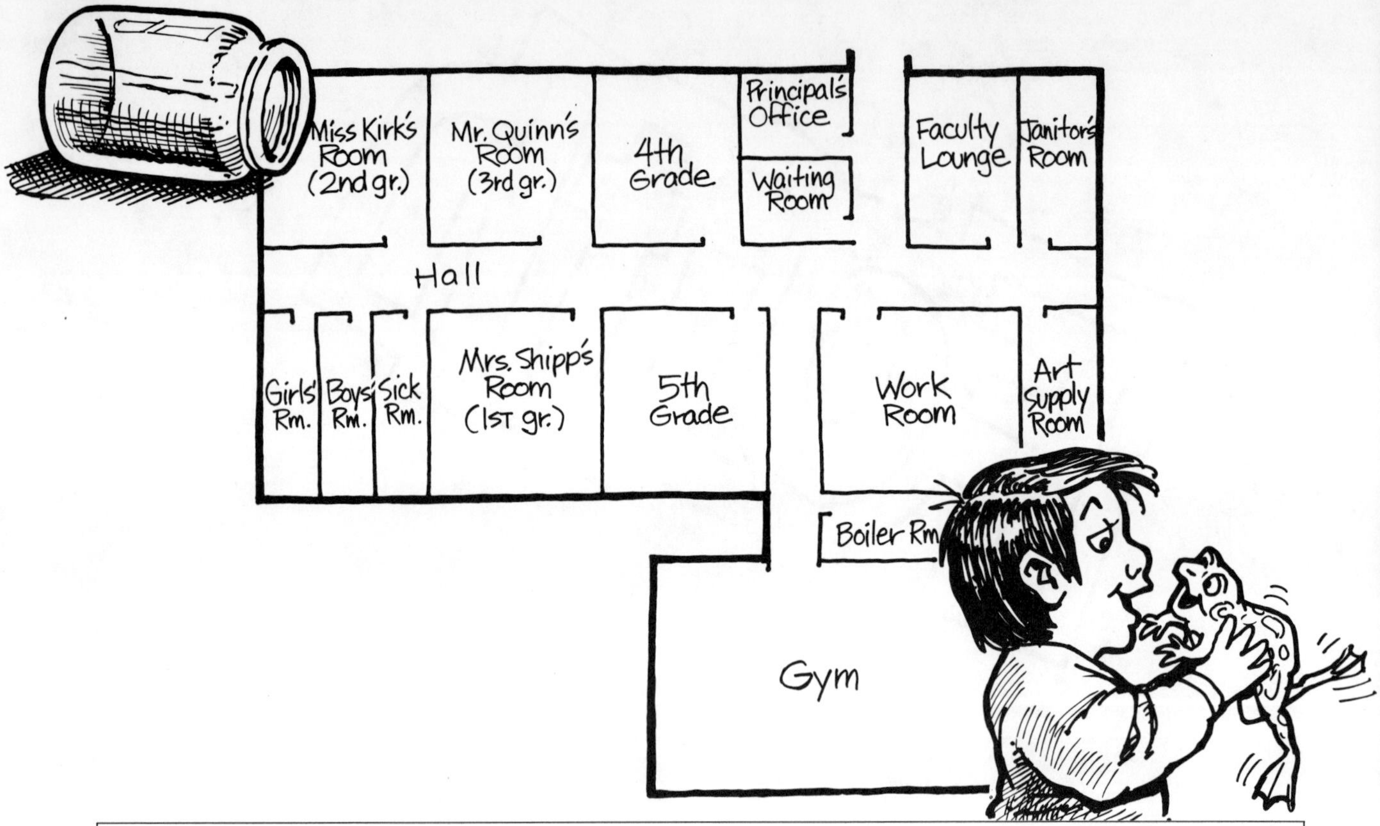

What if?

What if Frog had not been found? Would God still be God?

Would God still love the world?

Why do you think God sometimes says "No" to the things we ask Him to do?

Here is what I will do

The next time I am worried or sad, I ________________________
____.

They Did It!

1. This was it! Moses and the Hebrews and God were ready. The King had said, "Go!" And so they went. They left Egypt.
2. Once the Hebrews left, the King changed his mind again. He sent his armies after the Hebrews. God was watching. Moses knew that He was. He had faith in God.

   How do you know God was watching?
   How did God prove He was watching?

smelled	felt	heard

THINK ABOUT the sounds you would have ______________________.
the smells you would have ______________________.
the fears you might have ______________________.

THE FAITH THE HEBREWS PUT IN GOD SAVED THEM FROM THE EGYPTIANS.
THE FAITH WE PUT IN JESUS WILL SAVE US FROM HELL.

The faith Moses had in God showed by what he did.
The faith we have in God shows by what we do, too.

3. The ___ ___ ___ ___ ___ ___ feared the ___ ___ ___ ___
   16 5 15 16 12 5 — 12 15 18 4

   and put their ___ ___ ___ ___ ___ in Him and
   20 18 21 19 20

   in ___ ___ ___ ___ ___ His ___ ___ ___ ___ ___ ___ ___.
   13 15 19 5 19 — 19 5 18 22 1 14 20

Exodus 14:31b

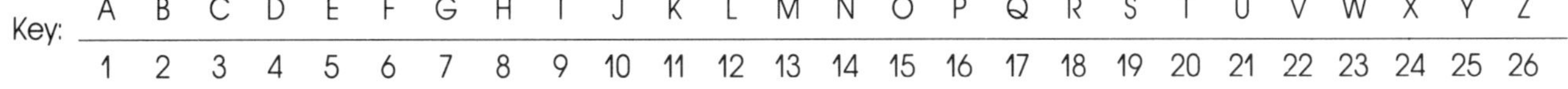

Key:	A	B	C	D	E	F	G	H	I	J	K	L	M	N	O	P	Q	R	S	T	U	V	W	X	Y	Z
	1	2	3	4	5	6	7	8	9	10	11	12	13	14	15	16	17	18	19	20	21	22	23	24	25	26

Showing Faith

Tambi shows she has faith in the branch when she climbs the

Mr. McShane shows he has faith in the seasons when he plants

Martin shows he has faith in the bank when he leaves his

How do we show faith in God?

... and, of course, by THINKING about Him!

The Gift

If I believe
And you believe
That we'll receive
The gift that we've
Believed God has
For you and me,
Then we have faith
In what's to be!

Thinking It Over

with Martin Magee

"What is the Gift?
A free pass to heaven.
Without the pass
I could not go there.
Here is why ..."

God does not sin. He is perfect.
I am not perfect. I sin.
No sin is allowed in His home, called heaven. Unless something is done about my sin, I cannot go to heaven. God has done something about my sin for me.

He sent His Son, Jesus, to earth to pay the bill for our sin.

When I tell God that I believe Jesus paid for my sin, God marks my sin bill "paid."

My faith in Jesus makes me look perfect in the Book of God.

"And perfect is what I need to be to get into heaven. God is in heaven. He paid my way to go there. I love Him for doing that. That is the Gift I have faith in."

GOD HAD A NOBLE THOUGHT WHEN HE PLANNED THIS GIFT FOR ME.

It is called ___ ___ ___ ___ ___ ___ ___ ___ ___.
19 1 12 22 1 20 9 15 14

Key:	A	B	C	D	E	F	G	H	I	J	K	L	M
	1	2	3	4	5	6	7	8	9	10	11	12	13
	N	O	P	Q	R	S	T	U	V	W	X	Y	Z
	14	15	16	17	18	19	20	21	22	23	24	25	26

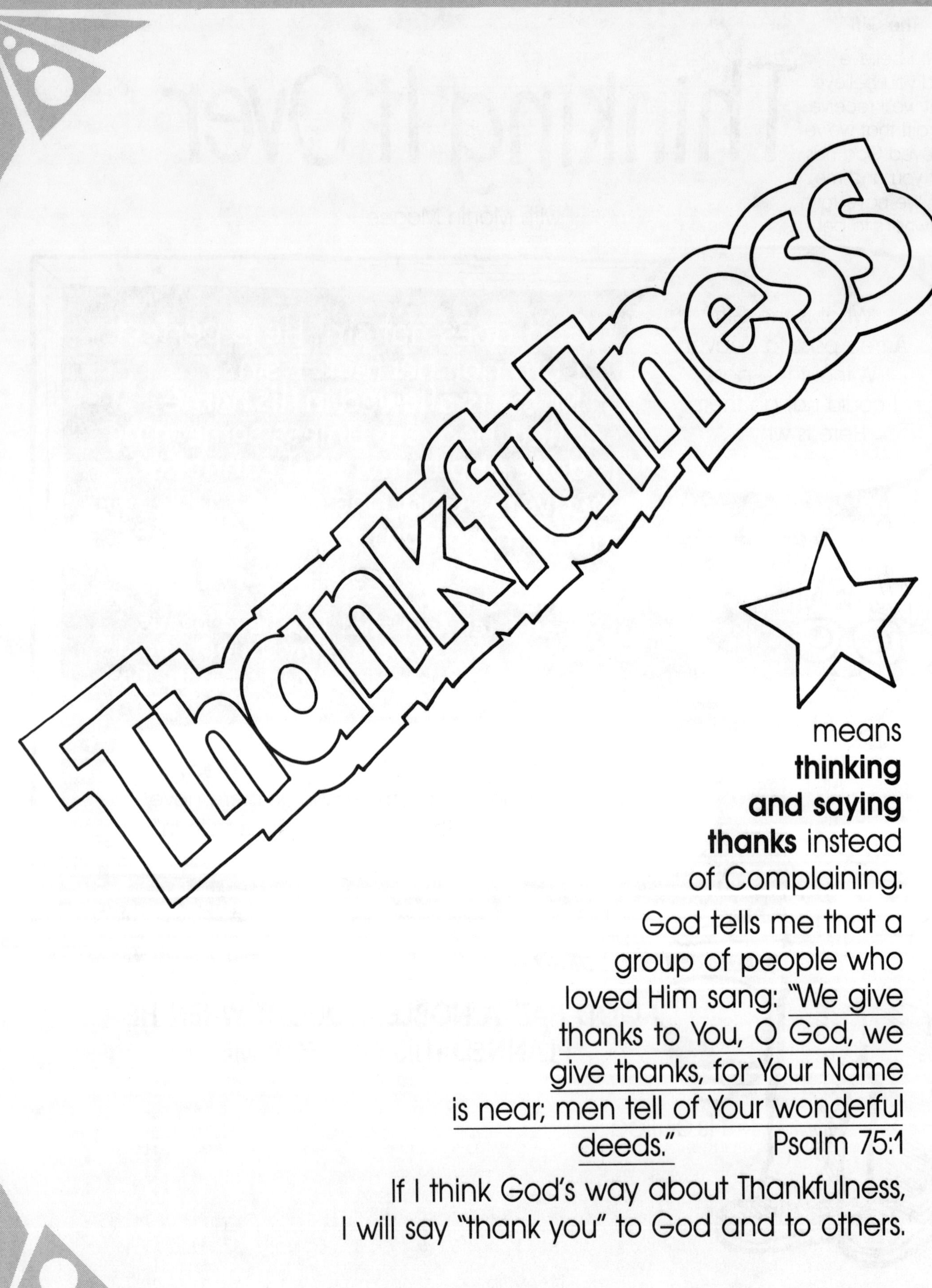

means
thinking
and saying
thanks instead
of Complaining.

God tells me that a group of people who loved Him sang: "We give thanks to You, O God, we give thanks, for Your Name is near; men tell of Your wonderful deeds." Psalm 75:1

If I think God's way about Thankfulness, I will say "thank you" to God and to others.

Thanks From A to Z

A B C D E F G H I J K L M N O P Q R S T U V W X Y Z

THINKING TOGETHER

Parents: We are "thinking thankful!" It is said, "He enjoys much who is thankful for a little." May we add the word "one" to the end of that statement? As you join your little one in thanks from A-Z, notice the things that make him/her special to you. Then do more than think thanks, say it. And while you're thinking thankfully, know that we are – for you. We are grateful for the chance to help influence your child toward God and right.

In our continuing study of Moses, we are seeing how he and his people said thanks. In our Sunnyview Story, we will find out how Patsy Lynn York handled a disappointment. Happy Thanksgiving!

The Rescue!

1. The King's army was chasing the Hebrews across the dry sea.
2. God was watching. When the Hebrews were on the other side of the sea,God rescued them. How? ______________________________
____
3. The hearts of the Hebrews were jumping with joy. They were happy to be alive.

   Think of the people cheering at a football game.

   There were more Hebrews on the riverbank than at any football game.

   Do you think they cheered as loudly as the fans at a football game?

   Do you think God enjoyed their cheering?

4. Moses sang a song of praise to God. It was a long song. Here is a tiny part of his song:
   "The LORD is a warrior;
   the LORD is His name.
   Your right hand, O LORD, was majestic in power.
   Your right hand, O LORD, shattered the enemy."
5. Miriam grabbed her [tambourine]
   and began singing and dancing
   for joy. The women joined her. They sang:
   "Sing to the LORD,
   for He is highly exalted.
   The horse and its rider
   He has hurled into the sea."

   Who made music? ______________________________

   If you had made music, would you like to hear people singing about you?

   Yes   No

MOSES AND THE PEOPLE SANG THEIR THANKS TO GOD. YOU CAN, TOO

A Sunnyview Story

What Do You Think the Snow People Looked Like?

What if?

WHAT IF Patsy had stayed pouty?
Jeanne had gotten upset with Patsy?

Here is what I will do

When I hope someone will come for a visit, but they can't, I will ______________________.

Thinking Right

Thinking thankfully
is terribly
Smart.
It thankfully changes
the parts that
Aren't.

What we think about is what we do.

THAT IS WHY THINKING RIGHT MATTERS.

My mind was thought up by _________ . Minds are _________ idea.

_________ knows how my mind works. He tells me to think right, so I will do right.

ONE WAY TO THINK RIGHT IS TO THINK THANKFULLY.

Pretend this is a Grumble. Grumbles make you grumbly.

Pretend this is a Thankle. Thankles make you thankly.

Grumblies and thanklies wait for you to tell them what to do.

If your mind grumbles, the grumblies take over.
If your mind thankles, the thanklies take over.

Grumblies make everything look bad.
Thanklies help things look better.

Patsy had the Grumblies. Then she sent them away with Thanklies.

It is more fun
to be with a person
whose mind
is filled
with Thanklies
than one
whose mind
is filled
with Grumblies.

God lets you choose what to put into your mind.

What will it be?
Grumblies or Thanklies?

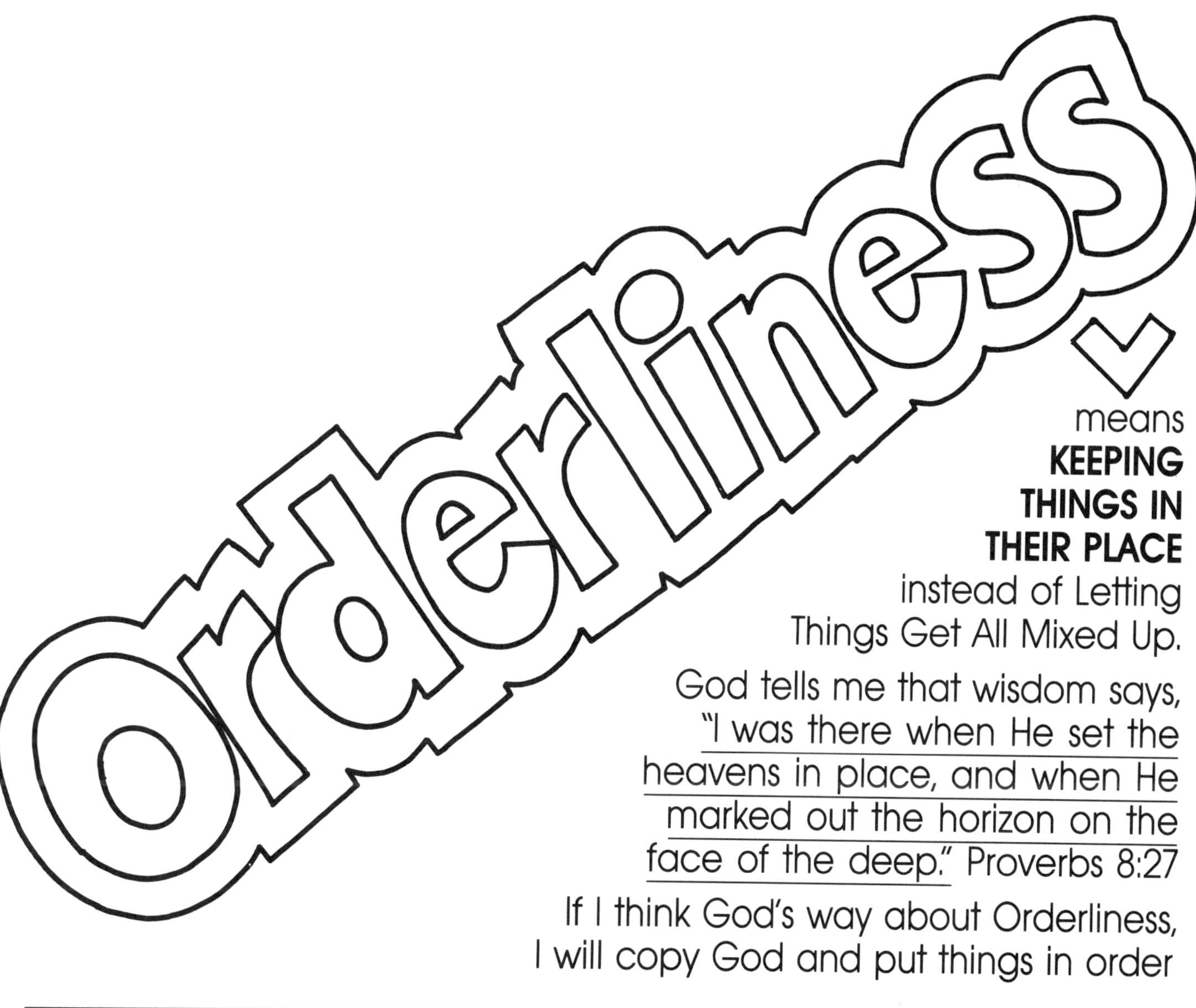

means
KEEPING THINGS IN THEIR PLACE
instead of Letting Things Get All Mixed Up.

God tells me that wisdom says, "I was there when He set the heavens in place, and when He marked out the horizon on the face of the deep." Proverbs 8:27

If I think God's way about Orderliness, I will copy God and put things in order

THINKING TOGETHER

Parents: Our focus is currently on orderliness. Wisdom was with God when He brought order to the universe. Wisdom will also help us plan our closets, our vacations, our desks, our Christmas gifts, our budgets, our everythings.

In our Sunnyview Story, Mickey Lee learns about orderliness the hard way. A look at Moses will give us instructions about orderly eating, and this month's poem hits on the frustration of a bedroom "gone wild."

If you have a drawer that needs straightening, this is a good month to get at it – with the help of your orderly second grader, of course.

The "Un-lost" Spaceship

Thinking back

____________________ got a
Mickey Lee, Donald

spaceship for his birthday.

His birthday was on

______________________________.
Saturday, Sunday

I think his spaceship looked like this: 

I think the spaceship was ____ inches long.

I think it was made of

metal ________

plastic ________

fiberglass ________

What if?

WHAT IF the desk had been orderly? How would his day have been better?

Here is what I will do

My desk and room will get messy fast unless I have a plan. Here is my plan:

1. ______________________________

2. ______________________________

3. ______________________________

Orderly Eating

1. The Hebrew people were in the desert.

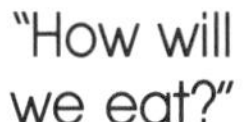

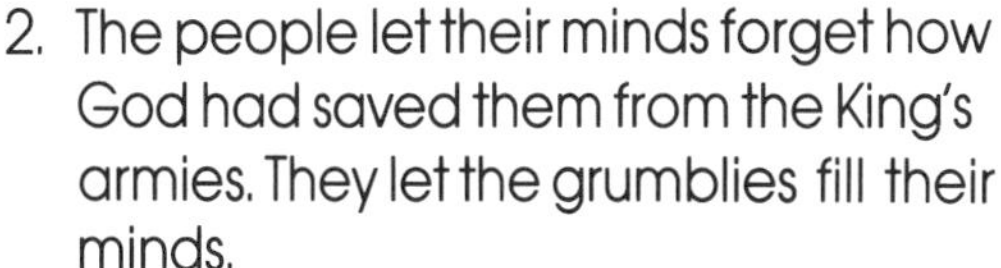

2. The people let their minds forget how God had saved them from the King's armies. They let the grumblies fill their minds.

   Let your mind take you to the desert.
   What do you hear? What do you see?
   Are you angry like the others?
   What are you saying to your friends?

3. They got mad at Moses. Moses said that their madness was really aimed at God.

4. God heard their grumblies. He was kind and fed them anyway.

   Do you think God likes to feed grumbly people ______, thankful people ______, or does it matter to Him?
   Yes ____ No____

   Which people would you want to feed? ________________________________

5. Every morning God filled their camp with dew. The dew would dry up and leave small breads that tasted like honey wafers. God called them "manna."

   Did the dew leave food at your house this morning? Why?

THIS IS WHAT GOD TOLD THE HEBREWS TO DO WITH THE MANNA. Put His words in order.

Gather twice as much on the sixth day.
Don't keep any of it until morning.
Rest on the seventh day.
Gather as much as you need.

First, God said ________________________________.

Second, God said ________________________________.

Third, God said ________________________________.

Fourth, God said ________________________________.

Signs of Order

Say the verse you are learning about orderliness.

Let your mind take you way back to the time when God and wisdom were making the world.

Pretend you are hearing God tell the earth what to do.
"Waves, you will stop right here."
"Birds, you can have the trees and the sky for your home."

Pretend God has asked you to make signs telling the earth what to do.

Make a sign for the waves.
Make a sign for the sun.
Make a sign for the birds.

Make a sign for the flowers.
Make a sign for the wind.
Make a sign for the people.

Do all of these things obey God's orders?

THOUGHT SPOT Room Gone Wild

I can't stand this mess
Another minute.
There's not an ounce
of orderly in it!

I wonder if God
Would help a child
Gain control
Of a room gone wild.

This is a room gone wild.

Please gain control of it.

How did you do it?

1. ______________________
2. ______________________
3. ______________________
4. ______________________
5. ______________________
6. ______________________
7. ______________________
8. ______________________
9. ______________________
10. ______________________

means
LETTING
OTHERS BE
SPECIAL, TOO
instead of Thinking I
Am the Most Special of All.

God says, "Honor one another above yourselves." Romans 12:10

Honor = Think highly.

Jealous = Being upset over someone else's specialness.

If I think God's way about MEEKNESS, I will be glad that all of us are special.

Above All, God

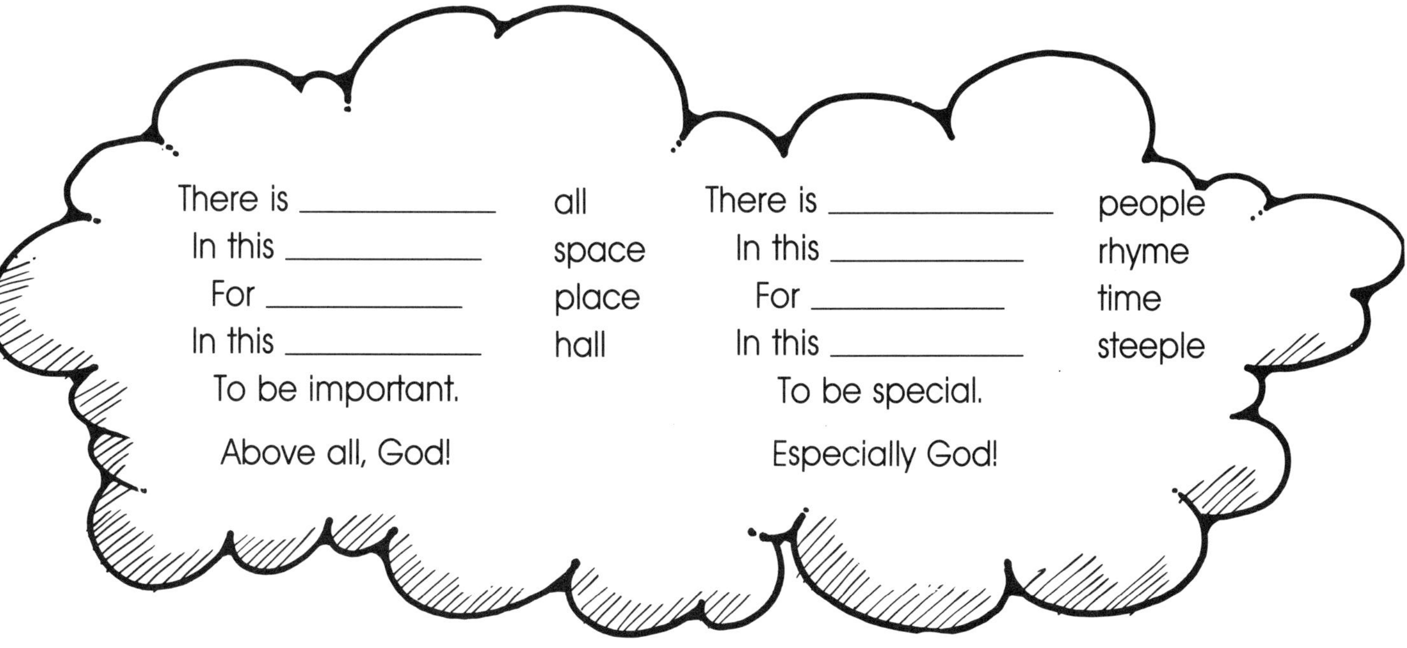

Thoughts to think

1. Think of God in the center of a Superdome. We are cheering for Him because He is so great.
2. Think of God talking to us. He is bringing each of His children to stand with Him in the Superdome.
3. He is telling all of us how special each person is that He has made.
4. Pretend we yell, "Boo!" to some of his children.
5. Pretend we make fun of some of His children.

How would God feel?
Do you think this is what happens when we get jealous?

THINKING TOGETHER

Parents: Meekness is being given the once over in our class right now. Our definition is, "Letting others be special, too." Meekness is giving others room to be what God has made them to be. It is doing what we can to show acceptance of their strengths and love in spite of their weaknesses. When we are meek, we are willing to share the spotlight. We are happy to serve.

Our study of Moses shows us his meekness. Moses is said by God to have been the most humble man on earth at that time. Moses served his people. Yet he was outspoken and became a confident leader. Our Sunnyview story features the twins sorting through meekness and learning to let each other receive praise.

Your child possesses such potential. We are happy to serve you both.

Meek Moses

A True Story BIBLE PAGE

Choose a picture to draw from this list:

- Moses walked up the mountain.
- Moses held his hands up in battle.
- Moses talked to his father-in-law.

Moses got water from the rock.

WHEN WE SEE OTHERS THE WAY GOD SEES THEM,
WE WILL SERVE THEM.

"Now Moses was a very humble (meek) man, more humble than anyone else on the face of the earth." – God

Two Special Twins

jealous poster piano

Marta played the ________________________ .
People said she played very well. Marta liked hearing them say so.
Is that wrong? Yes No

Berta made a ________________________ .
People said she drew it very well. Berta liked hearing them say so.
Is that wrong? Yes No

THEN WHAT WAS WRONG?

Marta became ________________________ .

Hum a little tune in your mind. Do you think Marta played that tune?	Fill in this shape with a color. ☐ Do you think Berta used that color?
Marta likes **MUSIC.**	Berta likes **ART.**
Which girl is a **MUSICIAN?**	Which girl is an **ARTIST**?

What if?

WHAT IF Berta had not been kind to Marta?
Berta had not made the poster because Marta would be upset?

Here is what I will do

Sometimes I don't want others to be special. The next time I feel jealous I will

____

________________________.

Thinking Pure

PURE means **PERFECT.** A pure thought is about something perfect. God is perfect. Thoughts about God, if they are true, are pure thoughts.

MY PURE AND PERFECT THOUGHT ABOUT GOD

means
doing right for someone I care about no matter what instead of Doing Right For Someone Only If It Is Easy.

God says, "Never will I leave you; never will I forsake you." Hebrews 13:5b

If I think God's way about LOYALTY, I will be loyal to people and things I care about.

Loyal Friend

Color this picture of T.J. and Donald.
Tell someone at home this story.
What ending to the story did you choose?

Thinking back

What if?

WHAT IF T.J. had been afraid to be loyal to Donald?
Donald had started to cry?
the older boys had tried to hurt Donald?

Here is what I will do

When someone is making fun of a friend I will ______________________

____.

We will stick together!

Signed: ______________________________

THINKING TOGETHER

Parents: We're taking a look at loyalty. T.J. gets a chance to show loyalty in this Sunnyview story.

In our study of Moses, we see him showing loyalty to both God and the Hebrews.

Loyalty offers us such security. It is one of the great feelings in life to know someone will stick with you through anything. You may want to sign the promise of loyalty with your child at the bottom of the page. There is room to even squeeze in several signatures.

God is loyal to His children. Let's be the same to those we parent and teach.

Loyal God, Loyal Moses, Disloyal Hebrews

The Hebrews were saying bad things about Moses and God again. Moses and God stayed loyal to the Hebrews anyway.

1. God said, "Get the people ready. In __________ I will meet with them."

   Think of it! How would it be if your city was going to meet with God on a mountain in 3 days?

   What would you wear?
   What would you be saying?
   What would you be thinking?

2. In 3 days, __________ led the people to God.

3. God used a loud voice to talk to them. They thought they were going to ______.

   There was thunder and lightning on the mountain and a ________ sound.

   God is so big and strong that a mountain cannot hold His greatness.

   God could have used His quiet voice, though. Why do you think He used His big voice?

4. Moses spoke to God for the __________. He was __________ to them.

5. God told Moses to tell the people His rules. The __________ of God are the ______________________________ of all.

   This is God's world.

   He can make any rule He wants to make.

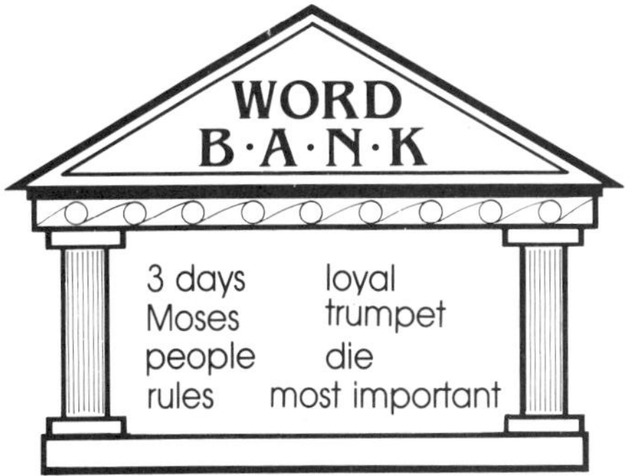

GOD DID NOT LEAVE
THE PEOPLE WHEN THEY TALKED BAD
AGAINST HIM.

GOD IS LOYAL!

What is the loudest sound you have ever heard?
When have you been the most afraid?
Do you ever feel afraid of God?

Let's Stick Together

Stick Like Glue

Stick like glue,
God and you.
He and I:
Loyal, too.

Stick like glue,
Me and them,
Us and you:
Loyal friends.

THOUGHTS TO THINK

1. Think about how good it feels to have someone stick up for you.
2. Think about how good it would feel to have the strongest man in the world on your side.
3. Think about how good it would feel to have the One who made the strongest man in the world on your side.

YOU DO HAVE HIM ON YOUR SIDE!
How does it feel?

means **Stopping myself before I do wrong** instead of Letting Myself Go.

God says, "He who guards his mouth and his tongue keeps himself from calamity." Proverbs 21:23

Calamity = deep trouble

If I think God's way about SELF-CONTROL, I will stop myself before I do wrong.

Hurt or Help?

Julia Mae has a problem.
She sometimes says things that hurt people.
Do you ever do that?
Words can 

. Words can hurt.

What do you think?

Did God think up the idea of words so that we can hurt each other or help each other?

Hurt each other ________ Help each other ________

THINKING ABOUT HELPING WORDS

Hurting words hurt us, so we won't think about them.
Let's think about helping words.

What words help you?
Who says them?

Think of some helpful words that were said to you today.

Think of some helpful words you said today.

WHAT CAN HELP JULIA MAE?
WHAT CAN HELP YOU?

THINKING TOGETHER

Parents: Self-control is our focus; self-control is our goal. But self-control can be tough. Our poem this month says so. Plus, we see the Hebrews lose control, as well as one certain someone in our Sunnyview story.

The rewards for self-control are enormous, both here and in the hereafter. Something this important needs strong exampling. Let's again pray for one another as we teach – and learn – this quality.

They Lost It

1. Moses stayed on the mountain and talked with God. Their talk lasted for over a ________.
   Moses was on the mountain 40 days and 40 nights.
   Count very slowly to 40.
   Do it one more time.
2. The Hebrews were at the bottom of the mountain getting nervous again. They began losing their ________ - ________.
3. They whined and made each other afraid. They came up with a bad idea.
   "Let's make a ______ of our own."
4. They asked Aaron if they could. He let his mouth get him into ____________.
5. He told them to bring all their ________ to him. He melted it and helped form a pretend god.
   What are you thinking about this?
   Were the people being loyal to God and Moses?
   Do you think this was a calamity?
6. The people did many ________ ________ with their minds and their bodies for their pretend god.
   Do you think the true God would ever ask us to do wrong for Him?
7. The people lost their ________ - ________ They chose wrong over right.
8. God could _______ what was going on. He told Moses.
9. God had given Moses a ____________ ________ for the Hebrews. The gift was a set of clay tablets that God had written on Himself.
10. Moses came down from the mountain. He saw the bad things that the people were doing. He became ________ ____ ________. Do you think it is right to be angry at wrong?

MOSES THREW THE SPECIAL TABLETS DOWN AND __________ THEM.

This was a sad day. Losing control always brings loss.

THE ONE IN THIS STORY WHO HAD SELF-CONTROL WAS ______________.

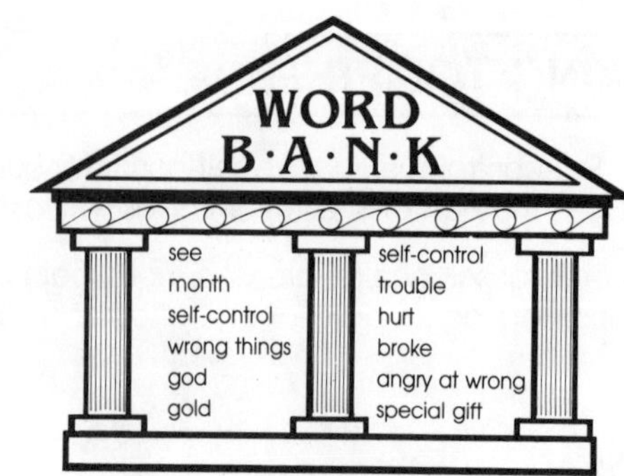

A Sunnyview Story

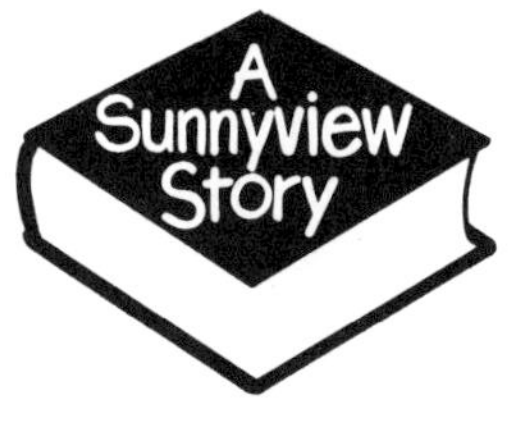

The Pinching of the Pincher

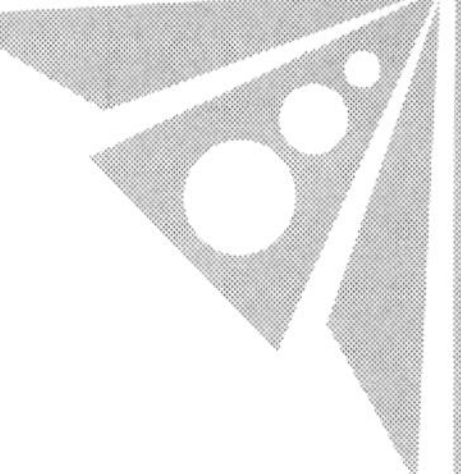

Who got pinched?

Whom do you think was the pincher? ______________________________

____

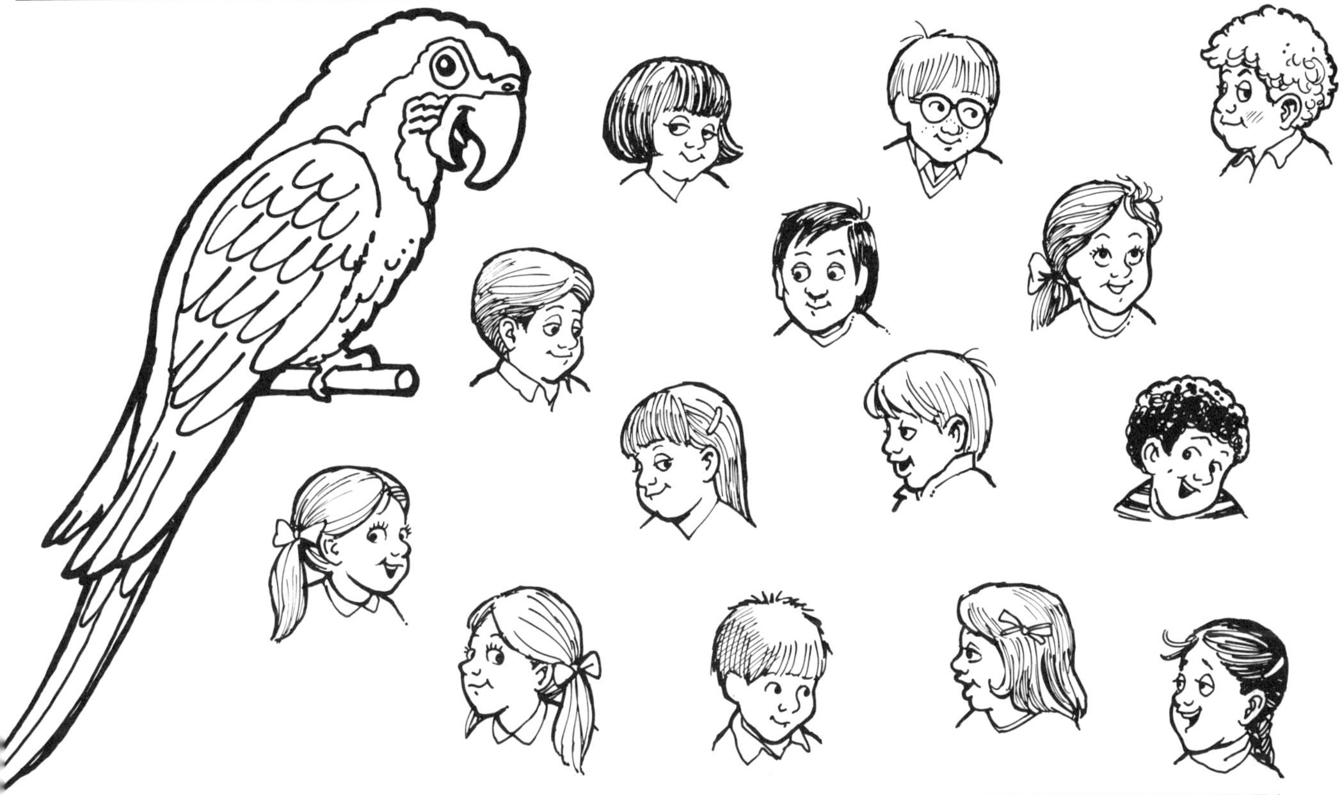

What if?

WHAT IF Adam had not brought the parrot to class? How might the pincher have been found?

Here is what I will do

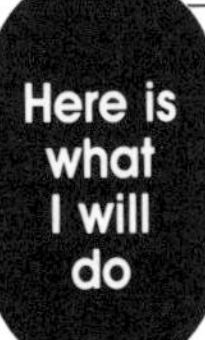

Sometimes I want to hurt people with my words or my body. When I feel like I want to lose my self-control, I will ______________________________.

Move Along, Wrong

Saying no to wrong
Is always right

Even if wrong
puts up a fight,

Even if wrong
Is out of sight,

Even if wrong
Begs all night.

Saying yes to right
Is never wrong.

So pack your bags
And move along, wrong!

A Thought to Think

1. Pretend that wrong is yanking at your sleeve.
2. Pretend that your friends are wanting you to do wrong.
3. Pretend that you say, "Yes."
   What happens?
4. Pretend that you say, "No."
   What happens?

Thinking Lovely

A lovely thought is a pretty thought. It is a thought about something – or someone – that is just right.

My Lovely Thought for Today: ______________________________

____

Do you think God cares how you choose?

means
**SAYING
AND DOING
WHAT IS TRUE,**
instead of Lying
by What I Say and Do.

God says "Do not lie." Leviticus 19:11

If I think God's way about
HONESTY, I will tell things as they really are.

THINKING TOGETHER

Parents: The quality we are now studying is "Honesty," a fitting companion to self-control.

This is a relevant subject to all of us. We will see Moses and God speaking honestly to one another, a scared but honest boy from the Sunnyview story speaking honestly to the principal, and an example of the trap at the end of every lie.

God says, "Do not lie." We tell the truth when we say we are encouraged by your support and faithfulness as parents. God bless you.

The Boy and the Arrow

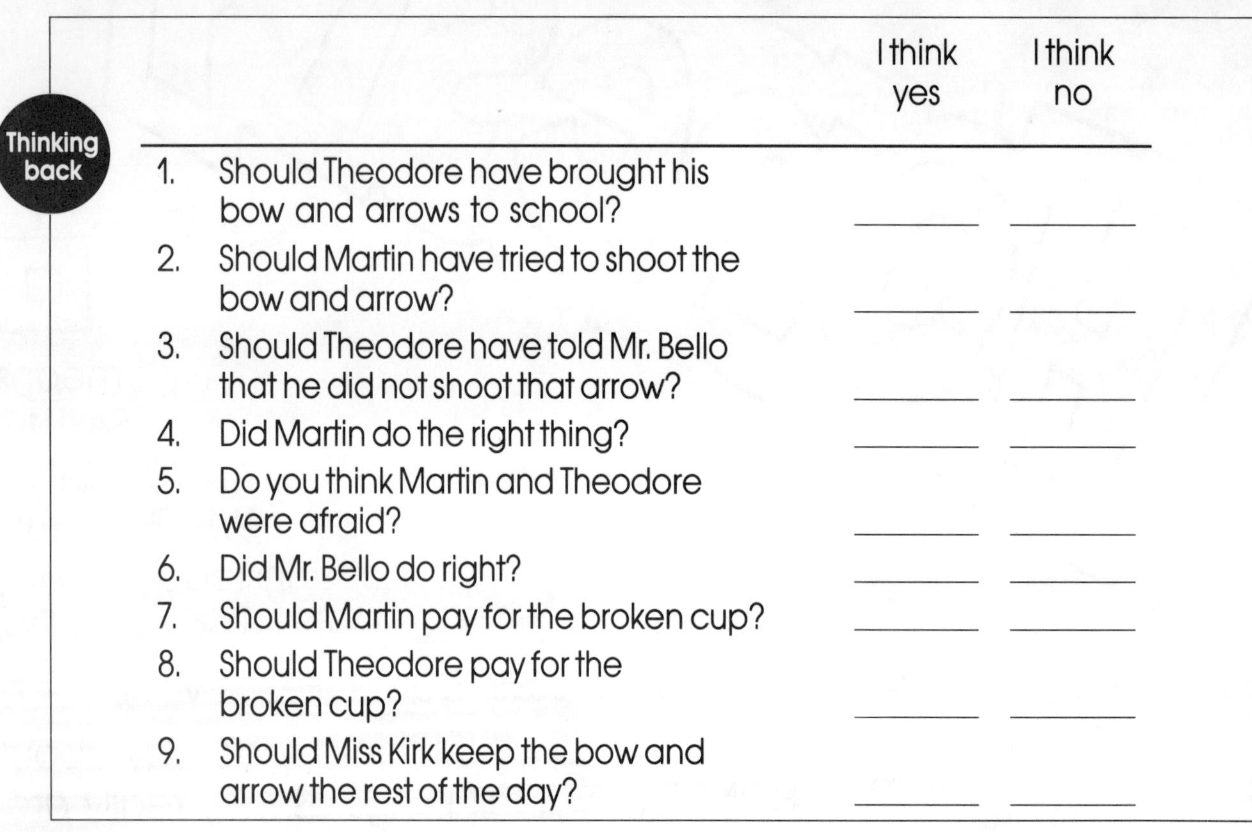

Thinking back

		I think yes	I think no
1.	Should Theodore have brought his bow and arrows to school?	______	______
2.	Should Martin have tried to shoot the bow and arrow?	______	______
3.	Should Theodore have told Mr. Bello that he did not shoot that arrow?	______	______
4.	Did Martin do the right thing?	______	______
5.	Do you think Martin and Theodore were afraid?	______	______
6.	Did Mr. Bello do right?	______	______
7.	Should Martin pay for the broken cup?	______	______
8.	Should Theodore pay for the broken cup?	______	______
9.	Should Miss Kirk keep the bow and arrow the rest of the day?	______	______

What if?

WHAT IF Martin had not told the truth?
Mr. Bello had punished Theodore?

Here is what I will do

When I do wrong and someone else gets blamed, I will ________________________________.

Truth Again

1. Moses went back to ________.
2. God and Moses spoke the ____________ to each other.
   God spoke the truth because He cannot lie. He is perfect.
   Moses spoke the truth because He loved God.
3. Moses asked God to forgive the Hebrews for making a ________________ god.
4. God ______________ them.
5. God wrote on a new set of stone ______________. What He wrote was truth.
   How long would you stare at something that God wrote with His own hand?
   ____
6. God's Word, the ____________, is true. Just like the words He spoke to Moses are true.

I AM SO VERY, VERY GLAD GOD DOES NOT LIE!

WORD B·A·N·K

Bible
tablets
forgave
pretend
truth
God

THINK ABOUT THESE WORDS

Here is what God said about Moses:

The __ __ __ __ (12 15 18 4) __ __ __ __ __ (19 16 15 11 5) to __ __ __ __ __ (13 15 19 5 19)

__ __ __ __ (6 1 3 5) to __ __ __ __ (6 1 3 5), as a man __ __ __ __ __ __ (19 16 5 1 11 19)

with his __ __ __ __ __ __ (6 18 9 5 14 4).

DO ALL OF YOUR FRIENDS TELL THE TRUTH?

God is your friend. What He says to you is true.

Key:	A	B	C	D	E	F	G	H	I	J	K	L	M	N	O	P	Q	R	S	T	U	V	W	X	Y	Z
	1	2	3	4	5	6	7	8	9	10	11	12	13	14	15	16	17	18	19	20	21	22	23	24	25	26

Tambi's String of Lies

Tambi's mom said, "Please fold the clothes on the chair before I get home tonight."

Tambi said, "Okay."

Tambi watched TV instead.

Mom came home. Tambi stuffed the unfolded clothes into her closet when she heard the car.

The Question	**The Lie**
Mom said, "Did you fold the clothes?"	Tambi said, "Yes."

TAMBI COULD HAVE SAID ______________________________

Mom said, "Where are my blue socks?"	Tambi said, "I don't know."

TAMBI COULD HAVE SAID ______________________________

Mom said, "They were in those clothes you folded."	Tambi said, "I didn't see them, Mom."

TAMBI COULD HAVE SAID ______________________________

Mom said, "Oh well. They'll turn up. I think this new top matches your red skirt. Let's look in your closet."	Tambi said, ______________________________ ______________________________ ______________________________

There is a trap at the end of every lie.

I Wonder Why

If God hates a lie
I wonder why I,
Who say that I love Him,
Would let one get by?

It seems such a waste
To let my lips taste
The flavor of something
The God I love hates.

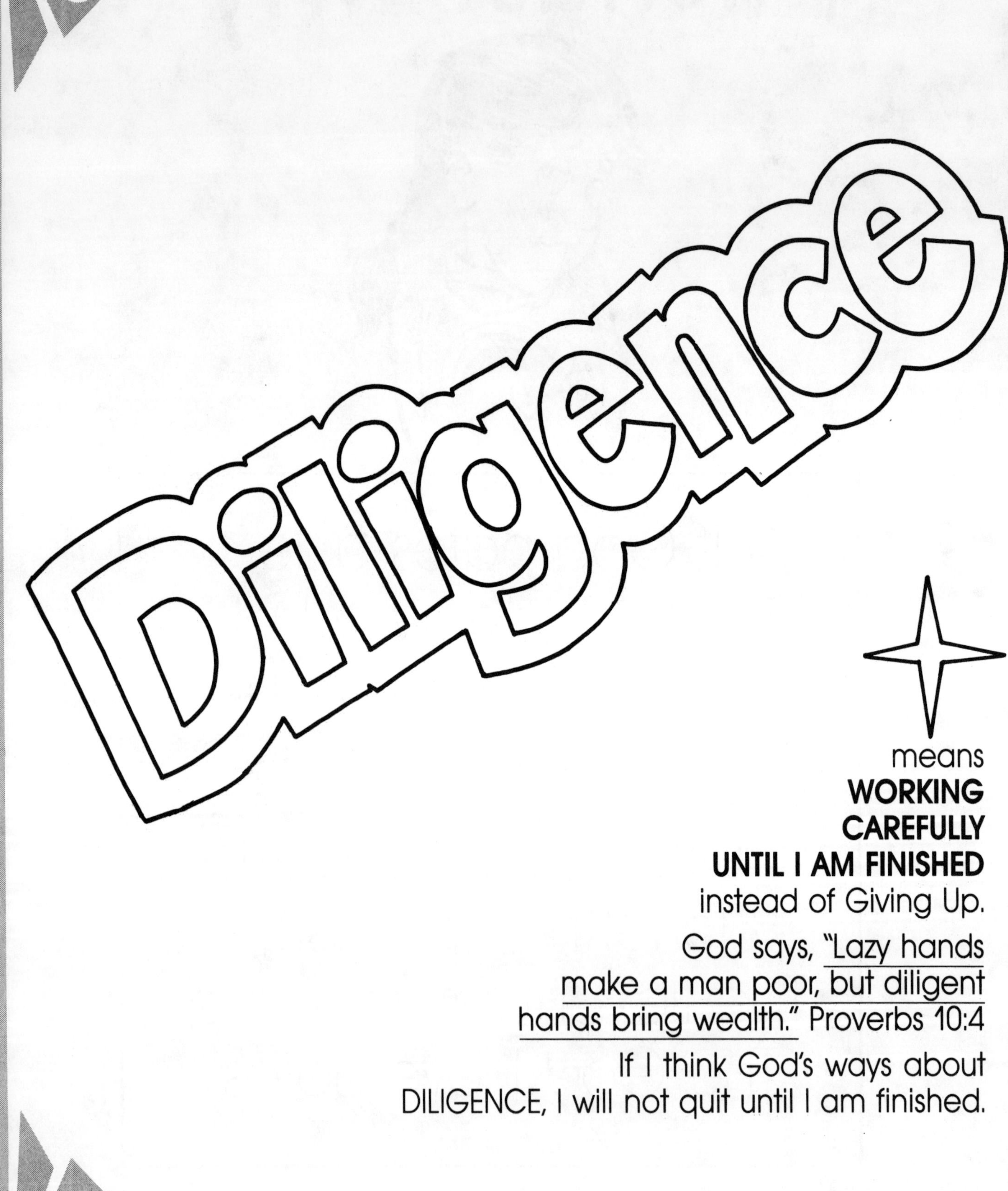

means
WORKING
CAREFULLY
UNTIL I AM FINISHED
instead of Giving Up.

God says, "Lazy hands make a man poor, but diligent hands bring wealth." Proverbs 10:4

If I think God's ways about DILIGENCE, I will not quit until I am finished.

Diligent Donald

These are the pieces of macaroni Donald used to build his amazing Macaroni car. What do you think his car looked like?

The Spies

1. The Hebrews wanted to go to their new land. They were getting close to the land God had told them about.
   How many times a week do you think the children asked, "How much longer, Dad?"
2. God told Moses to send out 12 men to look at the land. The trip was a secret.
3. The 12 sneaked over to the land. Big people lived on it. Would you have been worried if your dad was one of the men?
4. 10 of the men said,

   ____

   and 2 of the men said, ________________

   ____

   Who did the people listen to?

   The 10 ____________

   The 2 ____________

THE CHECKLIST:
What did their report say?
•PEOPLE: Strong or weak?
How many people? ____________
•LAND: Good or bad? ____________
Do the towns have walls? ____________
What kind of soil? ____________
Are there trees? ____________
AND DON'T FORGET TO BRING HOME SOME ____________!

This was another sad day for the Hebrews.
They chose not to trust their God.

BUT, two men were diligent. Who were they? ____________________ and ____________________.

HOW DO YOU THINK MOSES FELT?

THINKING TOGETHER

Parents: Diligence means "Working carefully until I am finished." There are many skills that require diligence for a second grader. Think back and try to remember what it is like trying to master math and reading and relationships. It requires diligence. God praised Caleb and Joshua for theirs. It is vital to encourage children in the same way.

Our Sunnyview story shows diligence in helpfulness, and we are learning to think diligent thoughts. Perhaps you'll see some of those thoughts in action at home. We're diligently hoping that you do and that you'll diligently heap praise on your careful worker!

A Sunnyview Story

Tie Breaker

Thinking back

When Suzanne was little, her brother told her that she couldn't play ball very well. Suzanne put that thought into her head.

She never tried to play ball again.

But Suzanne has a diligent friend. Her name is ____________________.

What happened the day of the school play-off?

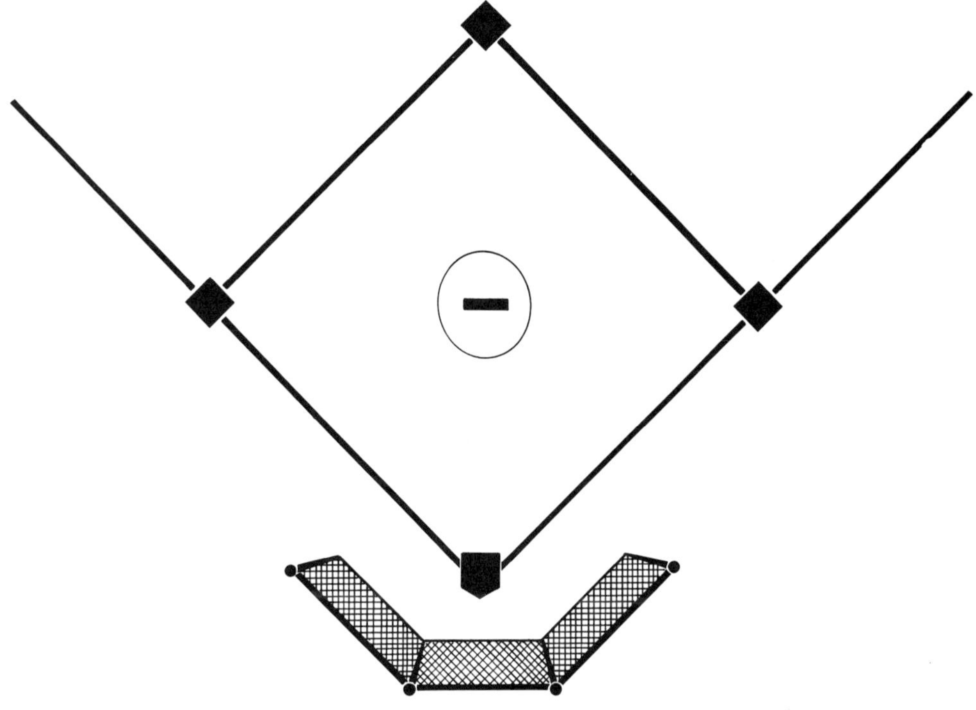

What if?

WHAT IF no one had ever helped Suzanne play ball?
Patsy Lynn had given up on Suzanne?
the class had made fun of Suzanne when she was trying to learn?

Here is what I will do

When a friend needs help, I will ______________________________

____.

I Can

I think I can.
I know I can.
You'll see I can.
Do what I can.

THOUGHT SPOT

If I think diligent thoughts, I will be diligent.
But, sometimes my mind gets thoughts that tell me to quit. I will cross those thoughts out of my mind.

Diligent Thoughts and Give-up Thoughts

- I can do it.
- People will think I'm stupid.
- No one will help you.
- If I need help, I will ask.
- I'll never finish the whole thing.
- I will do just a little bit at a time. It will get done.
- I will be a finisher.
- God is pleased with my diligence.
- God doesn't really care if I finish.

AN ADMIRABLE THOUGHT

God says to think thoughts that are ADMIRABLE.
What is **ADMIRABLE**?
An ADMIRABLE thought is a **SPLENDID** thought.

Here is one splendid thought:

Think of a job you finished.
Think of God saying, "Good work! I like the way you did that!"
Think of God saying, "I can count on ____________________ to finish a job well."

Can you think of another splendid, admirable thought?

____

____

____

____

means
WAITING WITHOUT COMPLAINING
instead of Wanting Things Right Now!

God says, "A man's wisdom gives him patience." Proverbs 19:11

If I think God's way – about PATIENCE, I will let wisdom help me wait.

THINKING TOGETHER

Parents: Patience is another one of those qualities that offers us a challenge at any age. Yet, when patience is demonstrated, it is a wonderful silent teacher.

In the story of Moses, we see the patience of God as He deals with more problems in the camp. He patiently works through the issue and offers a conclusion that the people can see and understand.

God is equally patient with us. Yet it is difficult for children to understand what patience is if they have not seen it in action. And that's the challenge!

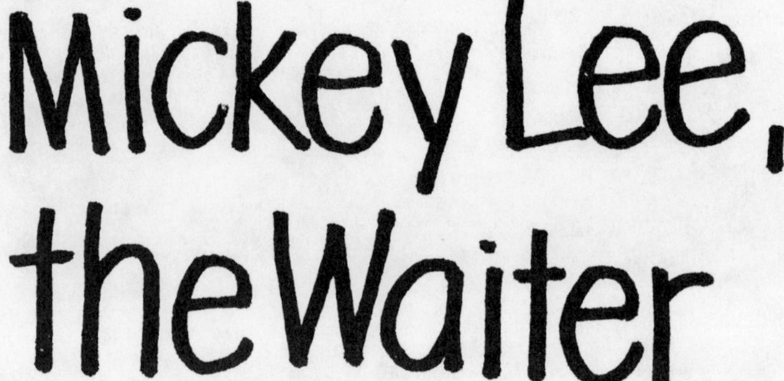

Circle the right answers

The day was Monday Tuesday Wednesday Thursday Friday.

It was the first recess second recess lunch hour.

Mickey Lee and Adam were in line for the slide swing tire.

Mickey Lee stayed left. Adam stayed left.

Mickey Lee got 3 turns got 0 turns.

Adam got 3 turns got 0 turns.

The same thing happened on the monkey bars, the teeter totter, and the four-square pad.

What happened the next day? And the day after that?

What was Adam's Problem?

WHAT IF Adam stays mad at Mickey Lee?

When someone gets mad at me for doing right, I will

____.

When I get mad at someone for doing right, I will

____.

The Patient Lesson

1. The priests were jealous. They wanted Aaron's job. They felt his work was more special than theirs.
   Let your mind put you there.
   What are they saying?
   How do their faces look?
   How do their insides feel?
2. God was tired of their grumbling.
   Is it okay to get tired of grumbling?
3. God could have lost his patience with them.
   Would that have been wrong?
4. Instead He told Moses of His plan to stop their grumbling.

THE PATIENT PLAN

6. buds	4. buds
3. tent	8. almonds
5. Aaron	1. 12
2. tribe	7. leaves

Gather ______ staffs,
(1)

one from each ______________.
(2)

Stand them in front of the ____________.
(3)

The staff that ____________ will belong to the priest I choose to serve Me in the tabernacle.
(4)

5. The next day Moses went to get the staffs.
6. Only one had changed. It was ______________'s.
   (5)

   But it had more than ____________. It had ________________ and ______________!
   (6) (7) (8)

Why do you think God let the staff do more than just bud?

GOD WAS PATIENT WITH THE HEBREWS.

God is patient with me, too.

7. Aaron kept his job as priest.

   What do you think the people were saying now?

How Patient Are You?

THIS MAZE TOOK ____________________ MINUTES OF PATIENCE.

It is Smart

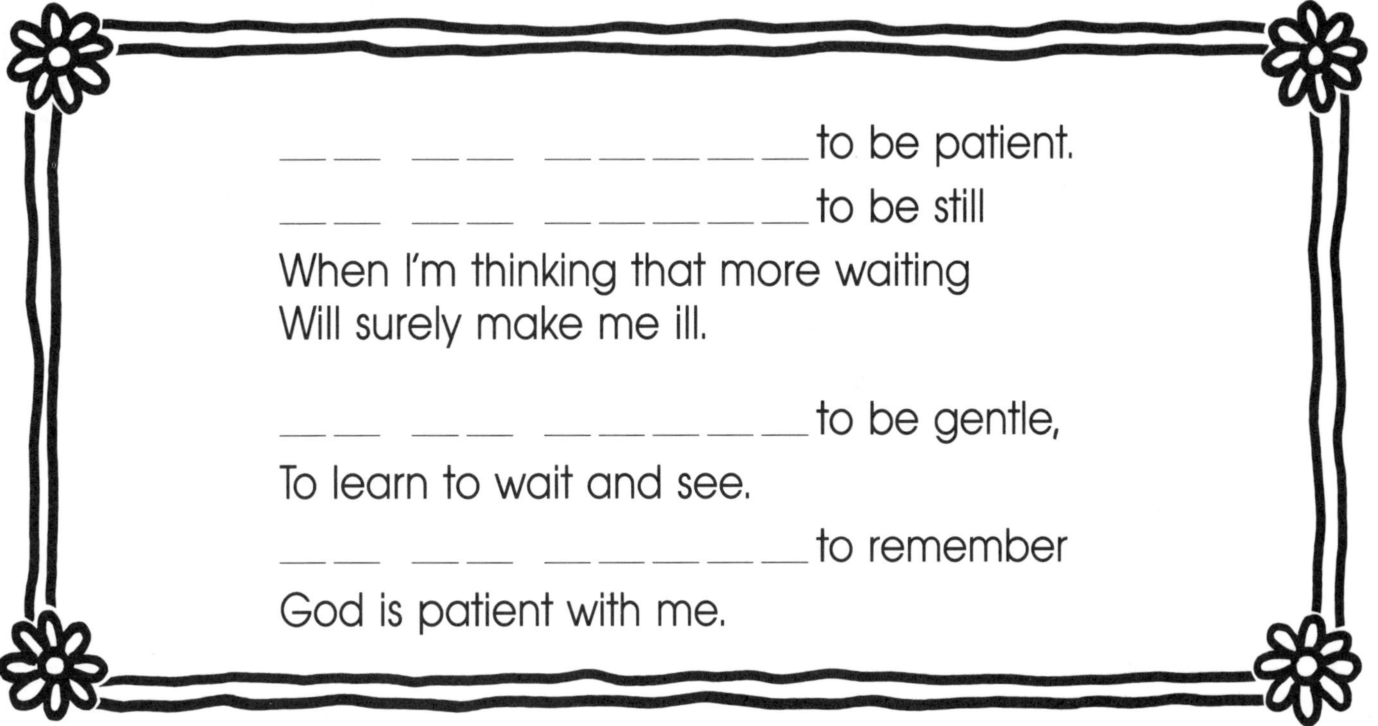

___ ___ ________ to be patient.
___ ___ ________ to be still
When I'm thinking that more waiting
Will surely make me ill.

___ ___ ________ to be gentle,
To learn to wait and see.
___ ___ ________ to remember
God is patient with me.

A THOUGHT TO THINK

Next time you feel like screaming, think of this:

Let your mind show you a picture of God screaming at you. Does the picture seem right?

Then let your mind show you a picture of God being gentle with you. Does this picture seem right?

Let your mind choose which picture to copy.

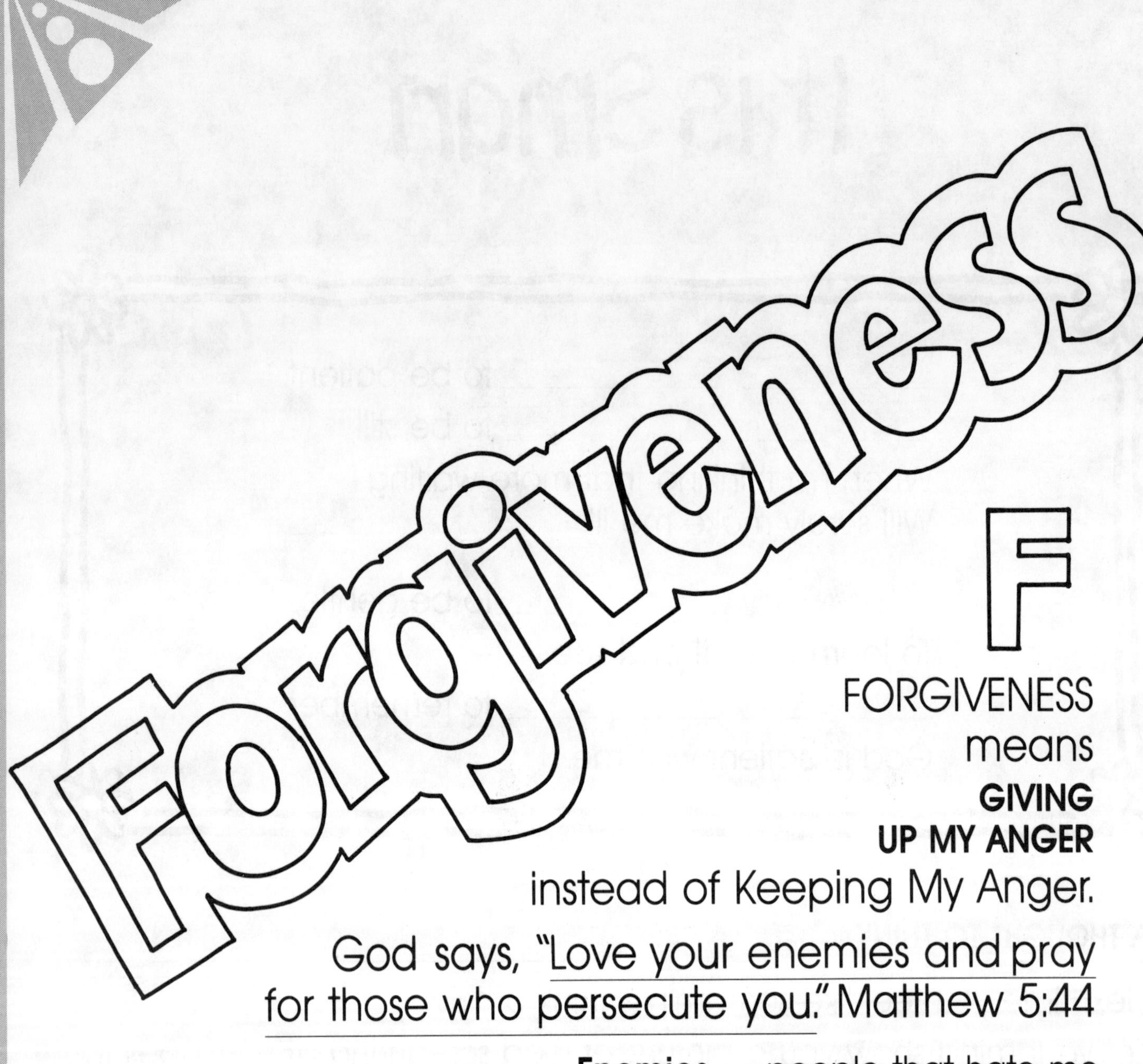

FORGIVENESS
means
GIVING
UP MY ANGER
instead of Keeping My Anger.

God says, "Love your enemies and pray for those who persecute you." Matthew 5:44

Enemies = people that hate me
Persecute = be cruel to

If I think God's way about FORGIVENESS, I will train my mind to give up my anger.

Anger - Keep it or send it away?

Anger takes the brightness out of the things I do.

Choose a color that seems ugly to you. Color it lightly over the pictures.

IS ANGER GOOD FOR ME?
IS IT SMART TO KEEP MY ANGER?
IS IT SMART TO FORGIVE?
What do you think?

THINKING TOGETHER

Parents: If we could get one message across to our children about forgiveness, what would it be? Anger is not worth it. It keeps us from enjoying the best of life and the best of God.

We will do children a great service by teaching them how to forgive, how God forgives, and how to admit wrong. In our Sunnyview story Adam continues to hold a grudge. In our study of Moses we see God forgiving Moses, yet the results of the sin remain.

Anger brings damage. Let's get rid of it!

Moses Does Wrong

1. The Hebrews were grumbling again.
   What were they saying this time?
2. Moses is tired of their grumbling.
   Would you be?
3. What did God tell Moses to do the last time the Hebrews were worried about water?
4. What did God tell Moses to do this time?
   ____________________ to the rock.
5. What did Moses do because he was angry with the people?
   Moses ____________________ the rock.
6. Did water come out from the rock? Yes No
   Do you think hitting the rock instead of speaking to it is a bad sin?
   Yes No
   Why do you think it was bad in God's eyes? ____________________
   ____.
7. God told Moses that because he did this he could not ____________________
   ____.

Do you feel badly for Moses?
Do you feel badly for God?

What if we could talk God out of His rules? Would His rules be true?
When have you talked your parents into changing a rule?

God is not like us.
He is God.
We must let Him be God.

Friends Again

As you color this page carefully, think about anger and forgiveness.

WHAT IF you choose to be angry?
WHAT IF you choose to be a person who forgives?

The next time someone treats me badly, I will__________.

God forgives
Because I'm His,
Because I've trusted
Jesus.

I forgive
Because I'm His
And like to do what
He does.

We Forgive

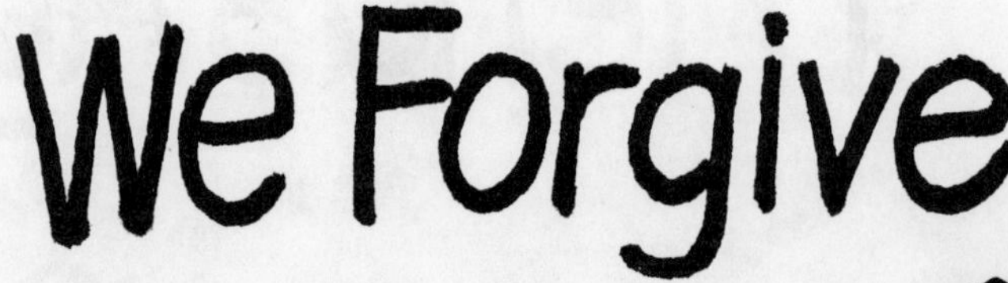

If Moses and you had a talk, what do you think he would say about forgiveness?

Will you enjoy talking to Moses in heaven?

What is one thing you might ask him?

Dear God,

Thank you for being a forgiving God. I want to learn to forgive, too. Please help me give up my anger.

Amen.

Signed ______________________

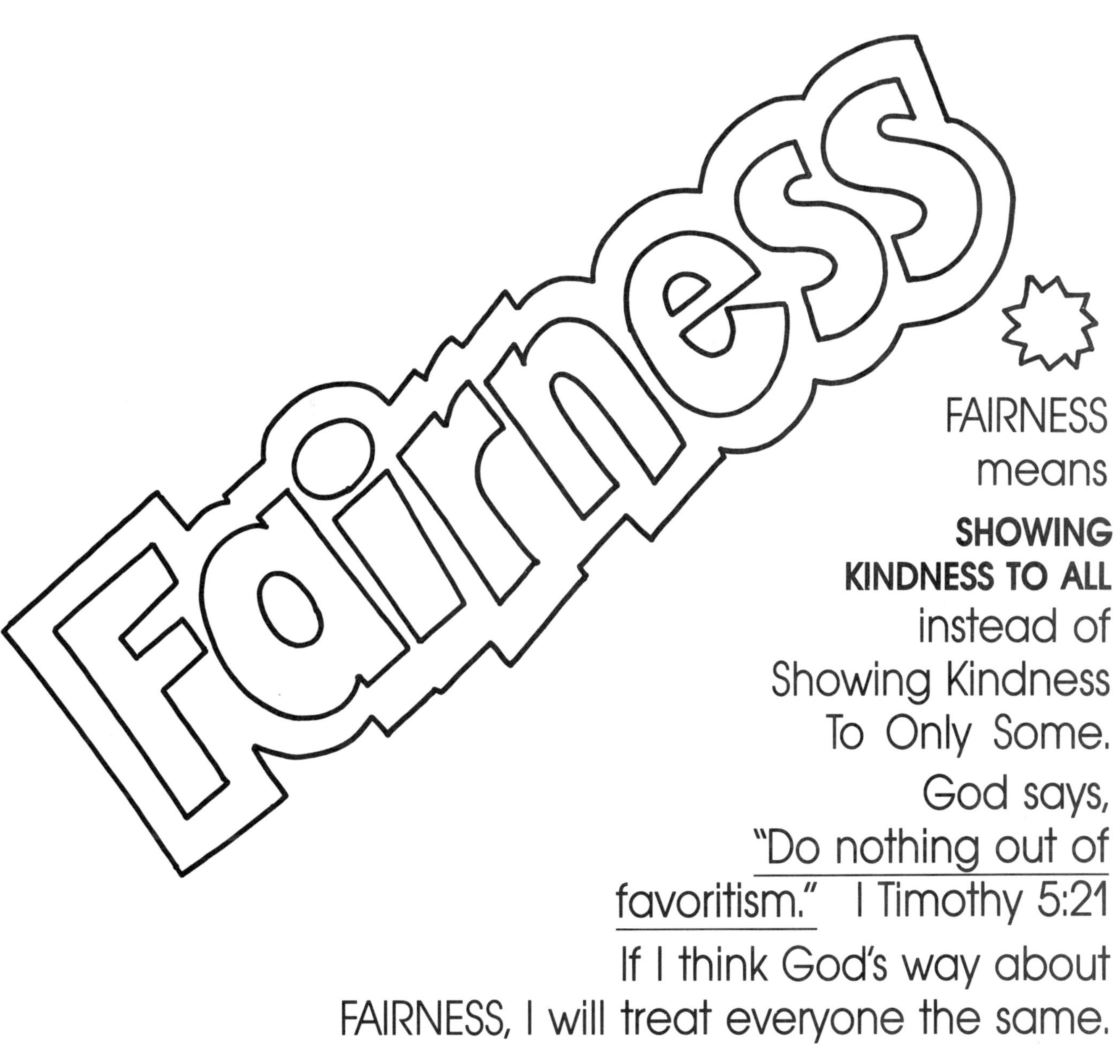

FAIRNESS
means
SHOWING KINDNESS TO ALL
instead of
Showing Kindness
To Only Some.

God says,
"Do nothing out of favoritism." I Timothy 5:21

If I think God's way about FAIRNESS, I will treat everyone the same.

THINKING TOGETHER

Parents: We are working through the issues of fairness. We see Moses and God being fair about dividing the land. In contrast to that, Julia Mae plays favorites and pays the penalty in our Sunnyview story.

Fairness is not always easily determined. There are many sides to a situation, and we each come to it with our own unique perspective. It is refreshing to know that God's perspective is always right, and He judges with perfect fairness.

That's Not Fair!

THINKING BACK MATCH-UPS

What did they say?

Julia Mae:	"Hey, that was in!"
T.J.:	"Out!"
Julia Mae:	"That's not fair."
T.J.:	"She wants the girls to win."
Donald:	"Out!"
Julia Mae:	"You need your eyes examined."
Adam:	"It was out!"
Julia Mae:	"That was in!"
Mickey:	"I'll show you what's out!"
T.J.:	"Out again! The girls win!"

What did they do?

Mr. Kirk:	pushed Julia down
T.J.:	screamed and hit
Julia Mae:	took sides
The other kids:	stopped the fight

What did the camera show?

Julia Mae   was fair   was unfair.

What if?

WHAT IF the camera had not been aimed at Julia?

Here is what I will do

When someone is unfair, I will____________________.

"Do nothing out of

___ ___ ___ ___ ___ ___ ___ ___ ___ ___."

6 1 22 15 18 9 20 9 19 13

When someone says I am unfair, I will____________________.

Key:	A	B	C	D	E	F	G	H	I	J	K	L	M	N	O	P	Q	R	S	T	U	V	W	X	Y	Z
	1	2	3	4	5	6	7	8	9	10	11	12	13	14	15	16	17	18	19	20	21	22	23	24	25	26

A Piece of the Land

1. The forgiven Moses was told by God to ________________ the land that would someday be the Hebrews' home.
   Think of what a hard job this was.
   What are the people saying about it in their homes at night?
2. The land was given to the _________ of the families.
3. One family had no father. Only ____________ lived in the family.
4. They came to Moses and said, "________________________________?"
5. Moses went to __________. Moses was ____________.
6. God said, "They are ________________. Give them a piece of __________, too."
   God gives special help to families without fathers.
   He says we should do that, too.

GOD IS FAIR.

He gives rewards to those that do right.
He takes rewards from those who do wrong.
He cares about the fatherless.

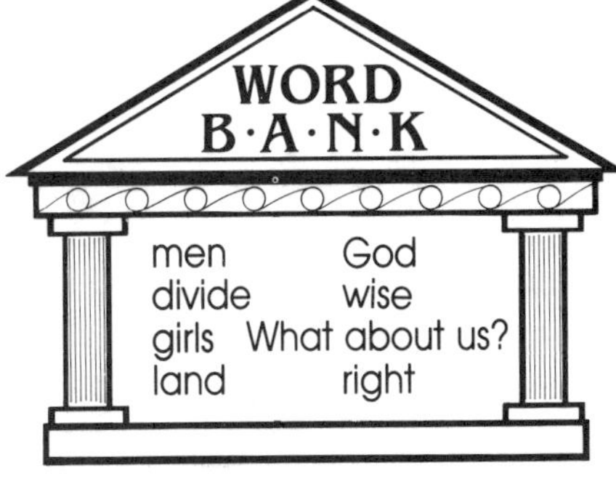

What if?

How would you feel if God played favorites?

Mad   Scared   Mean   Good

Fair Share

The kids are ready to eat.
You must cut the cake and divide the cookies fairly.
There are 8 people at your party.

How will you give everyone their fair share?

My plan: ____________________

____

____

Who Invented This Silly Game?

4. And puts me in an upset mood.
10. Let's play!
7. Of not playing favorites ever again?
1. Who invented this silly game
9. And puts me in the mood to share.
2. Of playing favorites? What a shame!
6. Who will play this wonderful game
3. It's mean and ornery and downright rude
8. It's kind and pleasant and always fair
5. I quit!

1. ______________________________

2. ______________________________

3. ______________________________

4. ______________________________

5. ____________________

6. ______________________________

7. ______________________________

8. ______________________________

9. ______________________________

10. ____________________

INITIATIVE
means
DOING WHAT I
CAN TO HELP instead of
Leaving the Helping to Others.

God tells me that Isaiah heard His voice saying, "Whom shall I send? And who will go for us?" And Isaiah said, "Here am I. Send me!" Isaiah 6:8

If I think God's way about INITIATIVE, I will see what needs doing and find a way to do it.

What Can I Do?

Jesus counts on me to do
the things He'd like
To do for you.

Jesus counts
On you to see
The kinds of things
He'd do for me.

Jesus counts
on us to know
The ways of love
He'd like to show.

THINKING TOGETHER

Parents: We are on the lookout for things to do! The Sunnyview crew found something worthy of their initiative. Moses had the initiative to make plans for a new leader of the Hebrews, and we are thinking about how to take care of one another.

We are having a good time!

New Leader

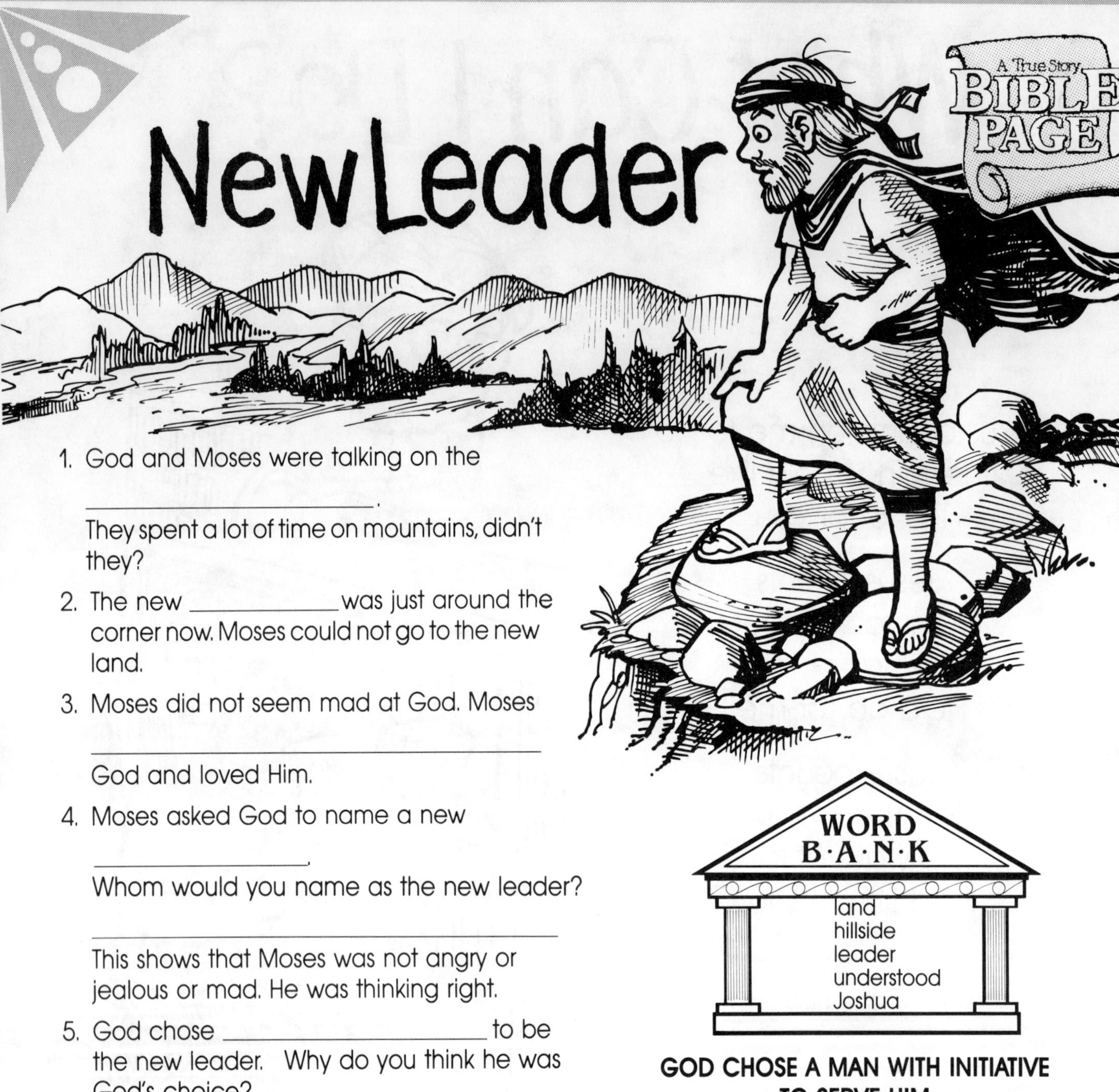

1. God and Moses were talking on the

   ______________________.

   They spent a lot of time on mountains, didn't they?

2. The new __________ was just around the corner now. Moses could not go to the new land.

3. Moses did not seem mad at God. Moses

   ____

   God and loved Him.

4. Moses asked God to name a new

   ______________.

   Whom would you name as the new leader?

   ____

   This shows that Moses was not angry or jealous or mad. He was thinking right.

5. God chose ________________ to be the new leader. Why do you think he was God's choice?

WORD B·A·N·K

land
hillside
leader
understood
Joshua

GOD CHOSE A MAN WITH INITIATIVE TO SERVE HIM

A THOUGHT TO THINK

Let your mind take you to the hillside. God is showing Moses the new land.
What do you hear?
What do you see?
What do you feel?
God did not change His mind about letting Moses go into the new land. He also did not change His love for Moses.

God's love stays the same.

Sh-h-h! It's a Surprise!

Adam Darby and Martin Magee had many items on their THINGS TO DO list. They showed their initiative by planning the party for Miss Kirk.

Think about the story. What do you think their TO DO list had on it? Who brought what? Who would do what?

Things To Do

If everyone brought 50 cents, and there were 14 people, how much money did Adam collect for the present? ____________

What do you think the class bought Miss Kirk? ____________________________

WHAT IF someone had slipped and given away the secret?

When I think of something that I can do to make someone happy, I will ________________________________.

Fill in the missing words

__________ __________

_________ _______ to do
The things He'd like
To do for ____________.

__________ __________

_________ _______ to see
The kinds of things
He'd do for __________.

__________ __________

_________ _____ to know
The kind of love
He'd like to __________.

WHAT WOULD GOD DO … for a person with a broken pencil?
WHAT WOULD GOD DO … for a person who just finished a race?
WHAT WOULD GOD DO … for a person with no lunch?

THINK OF IT! God says that each time you do something for a person, it is like you are doing it for Him.

Let your mind see you giving God a new pencil, a cup of water, and a half of your lunch.

It is so nice to have God in my life!

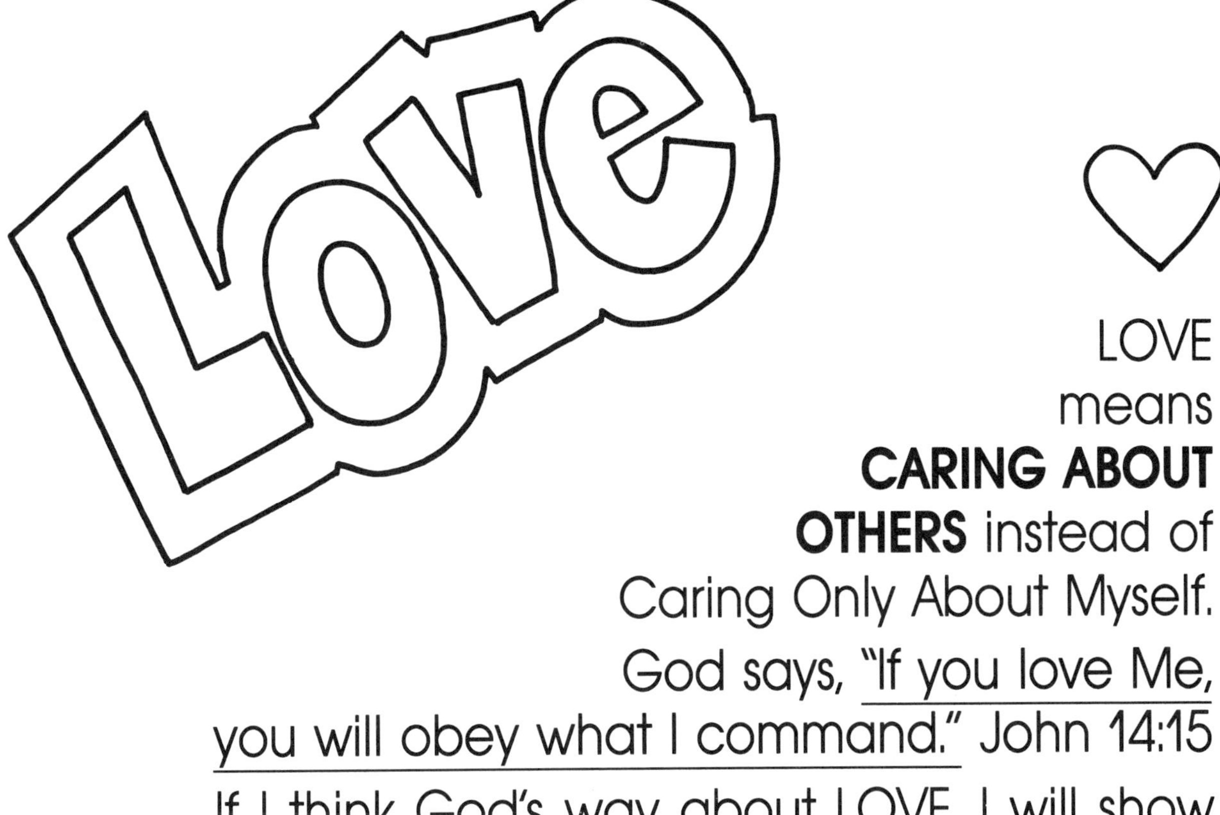

LOVE
means
CARING ABOUT OTHERS instead of
Caring Only About Myself.

God says, "If you love Me, you will obey what I command." John 14:15

If I think God's way about LOVE, I will show God I love Him by doing what He says to do.

THINKING TOGETHER

Parents: Love is on the agenda this month. God's brand of love – unselfish.

A new boy has enrolled at Sunnyview. He needs care,and Theodore is doing a fine job of giving it to him. Moses is in his final phase of leadership, and we watch in our minds as God buries His friend on the mountain.

Moses has showed his love for God through obedience. God looks for the same sign of love today.

From Moses, to Glenn Bender, to our class, to your child, and now to you. Love is all around!

Theodore Cares

Thinking back

Let your mind help you think like Glenn.
There are ______ months left of school.
You have just moved to town.
You are not with your parents.

What are your thoughts so far?

____

____

____

Your dad is in jail, and everyone knows it.
Your mom is in the hospital back home.
You are staying with your grandmother.

What other thoughts do you have?

____

____

____

Do you think Glenn needed to be cared for? Yes No
Why do you think he treated the kids badly at first?

____

Do you think Theodore ever wanted to give up on Glenn? Yes No

What if?

WHAT IF Theodore had given up on Glenn?
Glenn would have never been nice to Theodore?

Here is what I will do

When I want to show care for someone, I will ______________

____

Moses and God Cared

1. It was time to go into the land. Joshua and the people were ready.
   Were any of these people the ones who had thought the land was too scary for them?
   Yes **No**
2. Moses had to stay behind.
3. He spoke to the people about how great God is.
4. He sang a song of praise. The people listened.
   Was God listening, too?

   Let your mind put you there.
   What are the people saying?
   Is anyone crying?
   What are the small children doing?
   How does the voice of Moses sound?
5. God showed His love for Moses, too.
6. He took Moses to the top of the ______________________
   and showed him the land that he loved.
7. Then Moses died. God buried Moses there on the mountain.
   God and Moses had spent a lot of time on the mountain together. It was nice of God to let Moses' body stay there.

How do you feel about the story of Moses and God?

Love Cares More

My Secret Code

Every time
I do what I'm told,
I'm sending God
A secret code.

The message is,
"I'm loving you
By doing what
You want me to."

A THOUGHT TO THINK

Pretend that you have sent God a secret message of love by obeying Him.

- See Him reaching for it and reading it.
- Is He smiling?
- Does it make you feel good to think of pleasing God? Then be sure to keep doing it!

I was on the brink
Of learning to think
And now I can say
I'm thinking
God's way!

WHAT WERE THE TEN PLAGUES?

WHO PUT MOSES INTO THE RIVER?

HOW VALUABLE IS WISDOM?

HOW DID GOD FIRST SPEAK TO MOSES?

WHAT WAS MOSES' MOTHER'S NAME?

If my mind were a print-out,
What book would I be?
Would I be among the favorites
In God's library?

Title

Would He turn the pages slowly
and read every line,
Smiling at the way I've learned
To train my thinking mind?

It is best for me if I think God's way.
God says to think about things that are:

True Here is a true thought.

Noble Here is a noble thought.

Right Here is a right thought.

Pure Here is a pure thought.

Lovely Here is a lovely thought.

Admirable Here is an admirable thought.

Would He chuckle at my humor
And laugh at my jokes?
Have the angels read the parts
Where I obeyed my folks?

I have thought about it and here are my thoughts about funny:

One funny thing that happend to me:

____

My favorite joke:

____

____

____

One funny thing that happened to someone in class:

____

One thing that makes my teacher laugh:

____

I am glad God thought of letting us laugh.

I have thought about it, and I have gotten better about obeying.

I obey better about:

____

Here is what I think about obeying:

____

WHEN I OBEY,
I TELL GOD I ____________ HIM.

Would He gently mark the pages
That held all my prayers?
And underline the times I trusted Him
With all my cares?

Here is my prayer to God about THINKING:

FAITH MEANS ________________ ________________.

If my mind were a print-out,
What book would I be?
I'd want to be the kind of book
That God would love to read!

Here is what I like about me:

Here is what I think God likes about me:

Here is what I think about God:

The Sunnyview Crew

Here is what I think about the Sunnyview crew.

I think I would laugh the most with ______________________
I think my best friend would be ______________________
I think I could always count on ______________________
I think a forgiver would be ______________________
I think a person with self control is ______________________
I think I would like to share a toy with ______________________
I think I would like to give a party with ______________________
I think a diligent person is ______________________
I think the wisest person is ______________________
I think a smart person is ______________________
I think someone who obeys well is ______________________
I think I would like to help ______________________
I think an honest person is ______________________

MY CHOICE FOR THE THREE BEST SUNNYVIEW STORIES ARE:

1. ______________________ 2. ______________________
3. ______________________

I think the Sunnyview Crew showed me how to:

____

____

For one more look at a friend, read Mark 9:2, 3 and 4.